Bushwalking in the Mount Warning Region

Rob Blanch and Vince Kean

KINGSCLEAR BOOKS

First Pubished 1989 by Atrand Pty Ltd
Reprinted 1995 Kingsclear Books
36 Kingsclear Road Alexandria 2015
Phone (02) 557 4367

Printed in Australia by McPherson's Printing Group

Cataloguing in Publication Data
National Library ôf Australia
Blanch, R.C. (Robin Carlyle), 1944-
Bushwalking in the Mount Warning Region
Bibliography
Includes index
ISBN 0 908272 35 9

1. Hiking—New South Wales—Guide books
2. New South Wales—Description and Travel
1976—Guide books. 1. Kean, Vince,
1945— .II. Title

ACKNOWLEDGEMENTS

This book is the result of walking and camping experiences over a considerable number of years and we would like to thank the many people who have advised, assisted and encouraged us over this period.

Tom Tanner started it all by taking us to the site of the Stinson crash in 1973. He has walked with us on many occasions since and has been a great source of inspiration. Ian Greenhalgh and the Murwillumbah Library assisted with research for Part 1. Barry Hughes and Noel Tetlow read the first draft and encouraged and helped us. We are also grateful to Tony Groom who reviewed the manuscript thoroughly and gave us considerable constructive advice.

We would like to thank the National Parks and Wildlife Service for the use of their listings of flora and fauna of the region and Lawrence Orel, the Regional Media Officer for the Northern Region who helped organise the use of Geoff Biddle's photographs on the front and back covers. The Royal Botanic Gardens and the Australian Museum also assisted in the compiling of the scientific names. We would also like to thank the N.S.W. Forestry Commission. Thanks also to our meticulous editor Robin Appleton and to Catherine Warne for her enthusiasm.

We wish to record our thanks to all the people who have walked with us since 1973 and shared a common enthusiasm for the natural world. We value their comradeship highly. Finally we wish to thank our families who have given us the freedom to spend so much time in the bush and who have on occasions shared walking and camping experiences with us.

Rob Blanch and Vince Kean, 1989.

FOREWORD

One of the joys of travel is the chance to learn something about different places. An even greater joy can be to learn something new about your own backyard. The unexpected pleasure this provides can be compared with discovering some new dimension to a friend you have known for years. Such was the pleasure for me when reading *Bushwalking in North-East New South Wales*.

Although I have lived most of my life at Binna Burra such is the complexity of the natural history of the area that you can find something new to learn about it every day.

The Tweed caldera has always held a fascination for me because of its size, the geological story it tells and the effect the volcano had on the flora and fauna millions of years later. These stories are clearly told in this book.

Any visitor to this area, whether on foot or in a car, would find that this book will add immeasurably to their experience.

I commend Vince Kean and Robin Blanch on the painstaking effort they have made to produce this most useful guide to a unique area.

Tony Groom
Binna Burra
Lamington National Park

CONTENTS

PART III

BUSHCRAFT

TABLE OF ILLUSTRATIONS

Track maps have been provided for most of the walks. In the established National Parks excellent track maps are available and we have not attempted to duplicate them.

In the wilderness areas we have provided some maps for better known walks, but wish to stress that the maps are inadequate by themselves and need to be read in conjunction with the appropriate topographic maps.

1
Bushwalks of the Tweed volcano

People go bushwalking for many different reasons, some walk for the freedom and exercise, others walk for the satisfaction and feeling of achievement in covering large distances. Still others like to walk for the closeness to the environment and the delights that come when you reach a new understanding of the wondrous way that the natural environment works. Usually walkers spend years accumulating the kind of information that allows this type of understanding. This book is designed to supply some of the background information we have collected in the course of twelve years of walking. The suggested walks have a thematic approach centred around the inner remnants of the huge Tweed shield volcano.

The massive size of the Tweed volcano has created an environment that was, and is, incredibly diverse. At its peak the shield soared many thousands of metres above sea level. As the climate changed over time, the vegetation was able to adapt to the changing conditions by moving up or down the mountain. Today we see an unusually diverse environment created by the many niches left during the erosion of the shield, as well as the remnants of former vegetation types which the mountain has allowed to adapt and survive. Some of the rarest plants in the world are located in and around the area of the present-day erosion caldera, living fossils of bygone eras and climates long changed. Plants as yet unnamed and plants as yet undiscovered lie in this botanical treasure trove. The listing of sections of the caldera with the World Heritage Commission in 1986 is well merited and should provide some added impetus to the drive to protect and preserve this marvellous environment.

The bushwalks have been selected with a view to examining the range of environments produced by the volcano, and the intimate relationship between all elements of the natural environment. Some walks are quite arduous and should be attempted only by the fit and adventurous, but most can be attempted by the average person with a few hours' free time and the desire to do something interesting and satisfying. A four-wheel drive vehicle would free the walker from the vagaries of the weather but is not essential. Experience in walking and a copy of the latest topographical map may be necessary on some walks, but generally all that is needed is some form of transport, an inquiring mind, the time and the inclination. Each walk has been classified according to the degree of difficulty, the time needed, the distance and the advisability of attempting it in wet weather. We have also indicated when any additional equipment may be required or handy on particular trips.

The book is organised into three main sections. The first comprises background information on the structure of the Tweed volcano. Almost all the ecology of the inner volcano area can be explained in terms of the geologic units and their associated vegetation communities. Although not much detailed work has been done on this area geologically, we have collected the main ideas presented by work currently available, since we believe that this underpins any real understanding of the ecology of the area. The ecology of the area is then considered in terms of ecogeologic units. This term is used to cover the particular natural communities associated with particular rock types.

The second part of the book considers the various walks which can help to gain a deeper insight into the life systems that the volcano supports. In twelve years of walking we have covered all the walks suggested, but the interested person should be able to cover the walks in a few weeks, choosing walks that appeal and ignoring walks that duplicate experiences gained elsewhere. All the walks are aesthetically appealing and can be enjoyed as much by the leisurely stroller as by the serious student.

Where possible track maps showing points of interest and explanations of significant features have been included. The walks have been grouped according to their locality rather than their points of interest, as it is easier to locate a particular walk under this system.

The final section of the book discusses bushcraft and

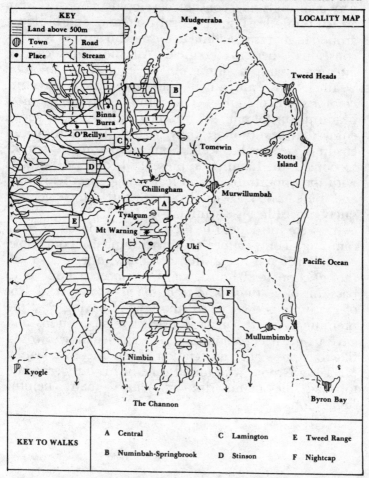

Fig. 1 *Map of the Tweed area showing the location of groups of walks covered in the text*

safety for the novice walker, as well as a discussion of equipment, and a suggested code of ethics for walkers in the area. The area is an extremely fragile environment, containing as it does so many relics of past climates and eras. Walkers need to be especially careful in their treatment of this unique environment. The area is also very small and under constant development pressure from agricultural clearing, chemical overspray and building around its margins, adding to the need to be preservation-conscious when in the field. All the walks can be attempted with a minimum of equipment in good weather, but we are convinced that a few modest creature comforts are desirable. The rainforest is at its most beautiful in the rain but a raincoat allows a walker to enjoy that beauty more fully. A little preparation can ensure an enjoyable walk. Some walks in the remote sections of the Lamington present ill-equipped walkers with the opportunity to do real damage to themselves, and some basic knowledge of bushcraft and elementary safety procedures is essential.

We were introduced to the bush by a master of basic camping, Tom Tanner of Murwillumbah. Tom's love of the bush and his ability to improvise were an ideal introduction to the area, and our sincerest hope is to pass this on to those who read this book. A special debt of gratitude is owed to all those who, having read the preliminary drafts, made constructive suggestions and gave us great encouragement. In particular we would like to express our appreciation of the interest taken by Mr Tony Groom who found time in his busy schedule to read the manuscript and make many helpful suggestions.

INSTANT GUIDE TO THE WALKS

The following guide contains the authors' suggestions regarding the relative difficulty of each of the walks described in the following chapters. The information is very generalised and is designed as a quick reference to assist you to choose walks suitable for your party. It is strongly recommended that walkers read the text thoroughly before the chosen walk is attempted.

Walk	Difficulty	Time/ Distance	Wet weather	Equipment
Mt Warning	Moderate	½ day 8.4km return	No	Drinking water & binoculars
Mebbin Forest	Very easy	½ hour	Yes	Meat for birds
Giant ironbark	Very easy	¼ hour	No	Camera
Brummies Lookout	Easy	½ hour	No	Binoculars
Amaroo walk	Easy	1 hour	No	Drinking water
Cedar Creek	Difficult	½ day	No	Map, compass & lunch
Stotts Island	Very easy	1 hour	Yes	Boat or canoe
Hellhole Falls	Very easy	½ hour	4 wheel drive	Swimming costume
The Cougals	Moderate	½ day	No	Drinking water, lunch & binoculars
Tomewin Rocks	Moderate	2 hours	Possible	Drinking water
Natural Arch	Very easy	1 hour 1km circuit	Yes	Picnic lunch

Walk	Difficulty	Time/ Distance	Wet weather	Equipment
Bushrangers Caves	Moderate	2 hours	Possible	Drinking water?
Mt Wagawn	Difficult	½ day	No	Drinking water, lunch & binoculars
Purlingbrook Falls	Moderate	2 hours 4km circuit	No	Picnic lunch
Best of all Lookout	Very easy	½ hour 1km return	Yes	Binoculars
Warrie Nat. Park	Varies	Depends on walk	Some possible	Depends on walk
White Caves	Moderate	3 hours 5km circuit	Possible	Picnic lunch
Daves Creek	Moderate	½ day 12.8km	Possible	Drinking water & binoculars
Mt Hobwee	Moderate	1 day 20.8km	Possible	Lunch & binoculars
Mt Bithongabel	Moderate	½ day 12.8km	Possible	Lunch
Mt Wanungra	Moderate	1 day 12.8km	Possible	Drinking water, lunch & binoculars
Echo Point	Moderate	1 day 17.6km return	Possible	Lunch & binoculars
O'Reillys to Stinson	Difficult	2 days	No	Full pack & maps
Wiangarie to Stinson	Difficult	2 days	No	Full pack & maps
Butlers Rd to Stinson	Difficult	2 days	No	Full pack & maps Permission
Stoddarts Rd to Stinson	Difficult	2 days	No	Full pack & maps Permission

Walk	Difficulty	Time/ Distance	Wet weather	Equipment
Westrays to Stinson	Difficult	1 day	No	Lunch & maps
Bar Mountain	Very easy	½ hour 750m circuit	Yes	Picnic lunch
Bush Camp Site	Moderate	2 hours	No	Lunch & binoculars
Blackbutts	Car park	View from car	Yes	Binoculars
Pinnacle	Difficult	2 hours 1.4km return	No	Drinking water
Gradys Creek	Moderate	4 hours	Possible	Lunch
Picnic area to Brindle Creek	Moderate	2 hours	Possible	Picnic lunch
Brindle Creek	Very easy	½ hour	Yes	Picnic lunch
Red Cedar walk	Very easy	½ hour	Yes	Picnic lunch
Mt Matheson	Easy	1 hour 2km return	Possible	Binoculars
Pholis walk	Easy	1 hour 2.1km	Possible	Binoculars
Flying Fox	Moderate	3 hours 9km return	Possible	Binoculars
Protestors Falls	Easy	½ hour 1.4km return	No	Swimming costume
Terania Creek	Moderate	3 hours	No	Lunch
Minyon Falls	Moderate	4 hours	No	Binoculars & lunch
Nightcap Track	Moderate	3 hours 5.4km	No	Drinking water & binoculars

8 WALKS' GUIDE

Walk	Difficulty	Time/ Distance	Wet weather	Equipment
Doon Doon Rock Spire	Moderate	2 hours	No	Drinking water
Big Scrub Reserve	Very easy	1 hour	Yes	Binoculars

PART I
THE NATURAL
ENVIRONMENT

2
Records in the rocks

The Tweed is an area of rugged terrain, large local relief and spectacular scenery. The area is dominated by a huge erosion caldera, the Tweed Valley, and remnants of the shield over 1000m. in altitude produced by a large and complex volcano centred on Mt Warning. This high land has not been cleared or developed for commercial purposes and contains the remnants of the natural ecosystems of the Tweed which are the setting for most of the bushwalks described in this book. A volcano of this size has extremely complex geology so the following description is of necessity highly generalised and aims to give a relatively simple basis of understanding for the interested bushwalker.

The volcano poured lava on to an ancient land surface composed of part of the eastern edge of the Clarence Moreton Basin. Over 20 million years have elapsed since the cessation of volcanic activity and erosion has cut right through the shield in places, exposing the older rocks of this basin. Some knowledge of the rocks of the basin is therefore necessary for an understanding of the geology of the Tweed region.

The Clarence Moreton Basin is a long trough with a north south axis extending from north of Brisbane to south of Grafton in New South Wales. This trough consists of metamorphic and sedimentary rocks. The oldest layers of rocks are the Brisbane Metamorphics Series which are approximately 250 to 500 million years old and outcrop on the eastern section of the Tweed

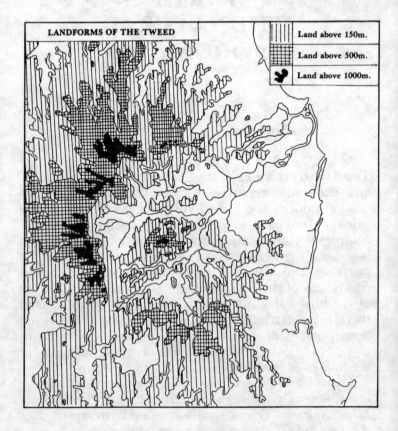

Fig. 2 Generalised landforms map of the Tweed
(Source 1:250,000 map of Tweed Heads)

Valley. The greywackes and phyllites occurring in this series of rocks can be seen outcropping in the headlands from Cabarita to Byron Bay. They also occur extensively in the Condong and Burringbar Ranges and on the lower hill slopes in the Tweed Valley east of Mt Warning, including the hills of Murwillumbah. When these rocks weather they form heavy red to yellow clay soils. The yellow earths are highly acid and support mainly eucalypt forest although patches of rainforest can be found in gullies or on sheltered southerly slopes. The phyllites have been extensively used in the valley for road-base materials and can be easily seen in the quarries around Murwillumbah.

Sedimentary rocks were laid down in the basin approximately 135 to 200 million years ago. Some of these can be found on the valley floor and the lower slopes west of Mt Warning. These rocks include the Bundamba Group, Walloon coal measures and Kangaroo Creek sandstones comprising claystones, sandstones, and narrow coal seams. The abandoned coal mine at Pumpenbil was a power source for the Murwillumbah Power Station formerly located on the site of the present Civic Centre. Some sandstones can be seen in road cuttings in the foothills, for example along the Numinbah Road. The sedimentary rocks also weather down into a highly acid podzolic soil that is somewhat sandier and poorer than the yellow earths. These soils mainly support eucalypt forests of which Mebbin State Forest is the largest remaining stand.

The metamorphic and sedimentary rocks of the Clarence Moreton Basin were separated by a thin and

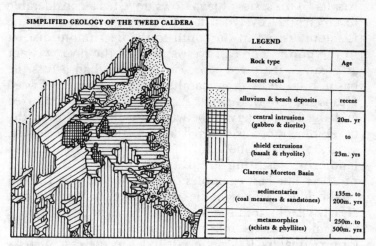

Fig. 3 A simplified map of the geology of the Tweed area

ancient band of volcanic rocks known as the 'Chillingham volcanics'. These rocks are highly weathered tuffs and rhyolites approximately 200 million years old and like the previously mentioned rocks in the basin dip westerly at an angle of approximately 45°. The Chillingham volcanics outcrop in a thin north south line interrupted by the Mt Warning extrusion and can be seen in the hills of the Chillingham area.

Approximately 23 million years ago, Mt Warning erupted and over a period of about 3 million years built up into a large and complex central volcano. A volcano of this size is created by many separate eruptions, punctuated by long periods of inactivity. Most of the volcanic material was extruded from a central vent located at Mt Warning, but several subsidiary vents also poured out lava at various times. These eruptions are best described in three phases, an initial extrusion of basalt, followed by a more explosive phase where acid material, mainly rhyolites, were thrown out, and a final quieter extrusion of basalt.

The first group of lavas have been called the 'Lismore basalts'. This series of lava flows travelled a considerable distance and covered a large area, extending from the Lismore district in the south to the Beechmont district in the north. The east west spread of the lava was not as great, as it flowed more easily along than across the basin, but the Lismore basalts are present in the Tweed Heads and Kyogle districts. Many separate flows occurred and the long intervals between the flows allowed the development of a weathered soil profile. Evidence of the separate flows can be distinctly seen in the terraced landforms resulting from the erosion of these soil profiles. The best examples of these terraces can be seen on the middle slopes on the southern side of Springbrook clearly visible from the Numinbah tick gate.

Lismore basalts are present as caps on the low hills (approximately 100 metres altitude) to the east such as Cudgen, Duranbah, Banora Point, Terranora, and

Tomewin. It is also visible at sea level at Pt Danger, Fingal Head, Cudgen Headland, and Cook Island. Lismore basalts form the middle slope above the sedimentaries but below the cliffs on the Springbrook, Lamington, and Nightcap plateaux. Basalts weather down into relatively neutral and highly fertile red loamy soils called 'krasnozems'. The basalt soils supported huge stands of subtropical rainforest, known locally as the 'Big Scrub', which included many fine stands of red cedar.

The volcano then became more violent and acid rocks were extruded, sometimes explosively, from the vents. Rhyolites, volcanic 'glass', agglomerates and tuffs were included in this group. The rhyolites are particularly resistant to erosion in this environment and can be seen as the cliffs on the high plateaux forming the western half of the caldera rim. Deep gorges have been worn in the rhyolites, particularly by the streams that flow into the Richmond Valley and into Queensland. Spectacular waterfalls can be found at the heads of these gorges where the streams plunge in the vicinity of 120 metres over the rhyolite cliffs. Imposing examples of these falls can be seen at Purlingbrook, Minyon, and Tuntable. Interesting rock overhangs sometimes called caves can occur beneath rhyolite cliffs especially where the rhyolite has covered a less resistant layer of tuff. Bushrangers Caves at the head of the Numinbah Valley are perhaps the best example of this phenomenon.

The final phase of volcanic activity was a relatively quiet series of basaltic lava flows. The rocks extruded during this period of activity have been called Blue Knob basalts and form a capping on the high plateaux of Springbrook, Lamington, the Tweed Range, and the Nightcap Range. Like the Lismore basalts on the lower slopes these rocks weather to fertile red soils that support dense stands of subtropical rainforest. Small relic patches of temperate rainforest exist on some of the higher peaks, and contain some of the northernmost examples of the Antarctic beech, usually found from Barrington Tops

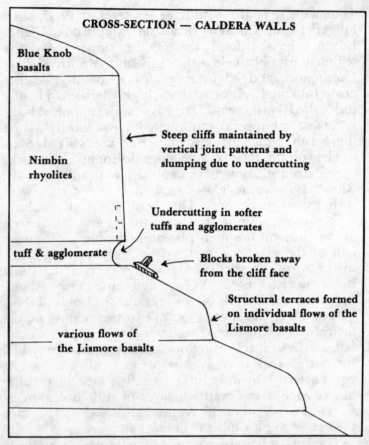

Fig. 4 Simplified cross-section of the valley walls showing geological relationships (A typical scene at any of the major waterfalls)

to the McPherson Ranges. These trees are among the most fascinating in the world. Their name comes from one of the three main groups of Australian flora, the Southern or Antarctic group. The Lamington area is perhaps the most northern occurrence of the Antarctic beech in the world.

Twenty million years of erosion has considerably altered the shape of the huge dome-shaped shield formed by the volcano. At first streams drained downslope, outwards from the top of the shield forming a radial pattern like the spokes in a wheel (see Figs 5 & 6). These streams gradually eroded valleys and deepened them with the passage of time. They soon cut through the Blue Knob basalts and began forming gorges and associated waterfalls in the rhyolites. Two streams that drained directly into the rivers on the floor of the existing valleys in the Clarence Moreton Basin, the Richmond and Nerang, cut down more rapidly because of their steeper gradients. These large valleys now separate the three plateaux bounded by rhyolite cliffs, and have become important transport lines in the area. However the stream that cut most quickly into the shield was the Tweed River, mainly because it drained directly to the sea and therefore had the steepest gradient.

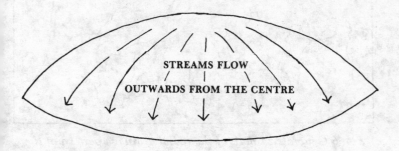

STREAMS FLOW
OUTWARDS FROM THE CENTRE

Fig. 5 Simplified diagram of the radial drainage pattern developing on the original Mt Warning dome

The Tweed has eroded right through the shield exposing the ancient rocks of the Clarence Moreton Basin. It has also extended its headwaters by cutting back into the central core of the shield and eroding concentric zones of weakness at the centre of the shield.

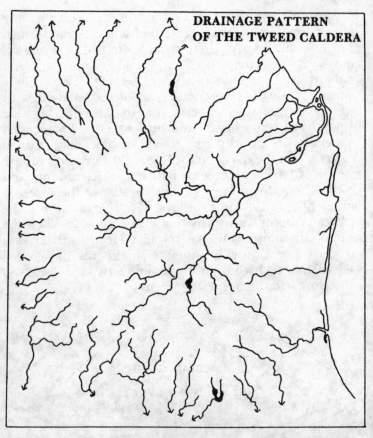

Fig. 6 Generalised map of the radial drainage pattern of the caldera, showing the Tweed system and the remnants of the old radial drainage system

In the process of doing this the Tweed 'pirated' some of the headwaters of the streams flowing to the north, west and south, and carved out the present-day erosion caldera, the Tweed Valley. It also exposed the plug or neck of the central vent, Mt Warning, and a series of ring dykes surrounding the plug. This ring dyke forms a chain of lower mountains surrounding Mt Warning and includes Mt Uki, the Sisters, and Brummies Lookout. It has also exposed part of the magma chamber composed of diorite, sometimes defined as micro-granite, which can be seen as rounded boulders or 'tors' on the lower slopes of Mt Nullum beside the Uki Road. Some secondary vents and dykes have also been exposed by erosion. These include the Doon Doon Doughboy, Dinseys Rock, Egg Rock, and The Pinnacle.

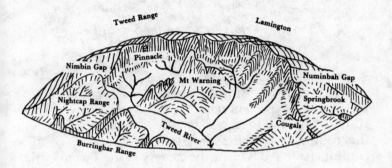

Fig. 7 The Tweed caldera now

The removal of large quantities of rock by erosion of the shield has resulted in a series of small rises in the land surface in relation to sea level as the Earth's crust has adjusted to the lighter load. This has caused the streams to cut deeper into the valleys resulting in a series of low river terraces in the upper parts of the Tweed Valley. One of these terraces is clearly visible in the Dungay area. The post-glacial rise in sea level resulted in the drowning of the lower part of the Tweed Valley, creating a ria similar to Sydney harbour. This part of the valley has been silted up forming a remarkably flat valley floor with numerous swamps. The flats extend upstream to Boat Harbour on the Rous River and to Byangum on the Tweed. This section of the river is tidal and has a muddy bottom in contrast to the rocky tracts upstream. The flats are also characterised by numerous swamps and an absence of river terraces.

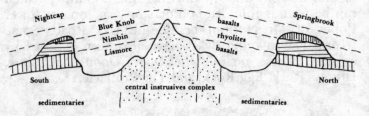

Fig. 8 Simplified cross-section of the Tweed Valley from south to north

This relatively simple account of the geological formation of present-day Tweed scenery gives some insight into the the great length of time involved and the complexity of the processes operating. It is this complexity that has made the scenery in the Tweed Valley unique in Australia, contrasting with the flat and relatively drab appearance of much of the rest of the continent. The size and stage of dissection of the caldera make it unique in the world, and the magnificent scenery compares favourably with more fashionable world tourist spots.

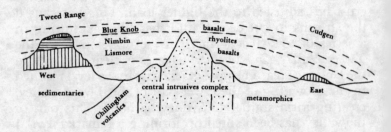

Fig. 9 Simplified geological cross-section of the Tweed Valley from west to east

3
The response of life

The Tweed volcano produced a sandwich of rock types. Within the volcanic rock series we have the Lismore basalts, the rhyolites and the later Blue Knob basalts (see Fig. 9). Associated with the rhyolites are various ash and agglomerate rock types resulting from the explosive activity normally associated with acid lavas. As shown previously these rocks represent different phases in the eruptions which created the shield. Below them are the weakly metamorphosed sediments of the ancient Clarence Moreton Basin. Each of these rock types is normally associated with a particular vegetation community.

At first glance the vegetation associations seem to be mainly related to altitude owing to the fact that there is a strong coincidental relationship between rock type and elevation. The main ecogeologic units are the basalts with their rainforests and the sedimentaries with their sclerophyll associations. The rhyolites resist weathering very effectively and therefore do not represent a large area mostly present almost vertical cliffs. Where weathering has exposed the upper surfaces these generally support vegetation similar to the sedimentaries, or in damp or fire-prone areas they may foster tea-tree heath associations.

Factors other than rock type may have importance in localised pockets. The northeast slopes of hills generally receive more sunlight and the southwest slopes tend to be more protected and damp. Pockets of alluvial soil in protected areas may support rainforest in unlikely areas. Fire is a major factor in the location of rainforests. Areas protected from fire may carry rainforest. In fact it is quite readily accepted in expert circles that rainforests continue to exist in places such as the Tweed only in areas where fire is excluded. Such areas are termed 'fire refuges'.

Within the erosion caldera the chief fire refuges are the higher areas where rainfall maintains abundant supplies of water, and the lowlands where high water tables keep ground fires to a minimum. In both cases the rainforest helps create and maintain the humidity by excluding sunlight from the ground and eliminating wind, thus reducing evaporation. Additionally the soils in both areas contain large amounts of material of basaltic origin which has good water-retaining capabilities.

The rhyolite areas have two factors mitigating against the retention of water in the soil. Firstly the rhyolites have resisted erosion and have maintained steep slopes, often sheer cliffs, which encourage rapid runoff and limit the development of deep soils. Secondly, the rhyolites weather to a sandy type of soil which is very permeable and has little water-retention capability. Where rhyolites are exposed as at Daves Creek near Binna Burra, the Tweed Pinnacle or the Doon Doon saddle rainforest associations are conspicuously absent, and a species of poor heath-type vegetation is dominant. For those who care to try, one of the tea-trees usually found in these locations is the lemon-scented tea-tree which, when its leaves are boiled in the billy, provides a most refreshing 'cuppa'.

The basement rocks of the Clarence Moreton Series and the Brisbane Metamorphics Series weather to a soil rich in clay. Since they were water-borne sediments they contain much clay and the soils that they create are dominated by the clay fraction. The poor podzolic soils developed upon them will not retain water usable to plants, and cannot support a diverse flora. The dry sclerophyll associations they support produce leaf litter that resists breaking down and builds up as 'fuel' on the forest floor encouraging ground fires. This causes a lack of humus in the soil and humus increases the capacity of the soil to hold water. The baking effect of intense ground fires may also reduce the soil's capacity to infiltrate and retain water.

FLOOD-PLAIN FORESTS

The floor of the Tweed Valley contained a variety of plant communities, but most of this has been cleared and drained for development. Only one substantial remnant of the former communities remains on Stotts Island, a small island in the Tweed River between Chinderah and Tumbulgum. A study of this island and its vegetation enables us to reconstruct the former vegetation pattern of the valley floor. The distribution of the various plant communities is strongly dependent on drainage, with subtropical rainforest growing on the higher well-drained ground of natural levees and river terraces. This lowland rainforest was the most luxurious and complex in the valley, containing over 400 separate tree species.

The rainforest gives way to less complex forest in lower, less well-drained circumstances. Palm glades dominated by bangalow palms separated the rainforests from the swamp forests. Stands of magnificent hoop pines tend

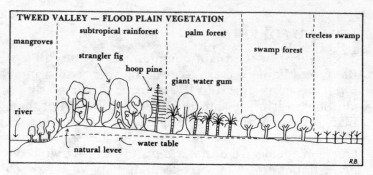

Fig. 10 Simplified cross-section of the valley floor showing the relationship between vegetation and micro-relief (Based on studies of Stotts Island)

to grow in the transition zone between the rainforests and the palm glades. These huge trees are readily visible on Stotts Island and can be seen clearly, emerging above the canopy, as you drive along the Pacific Highway.

Three types of swamp forests grew in the numerous swamps that existed on the flood plain. Their distribution was related to the salinity of the water in the swamps. Swamps that were inundated regularly by sea water at high tide supported mangroves. Fresh-water swamps were covered by tea-tree forests. Intermediate areas were covered by she-oak forests which show some tolerance of brackish conditions. Some swamps are treeless as they are too deep to support tree growth, instead they support a swamp grass community.

Stotts Island functions as a living 'museum' as it preserves small communities of all these types of vegetation. Some depauperate patches (see glossary) of these communities exist in other parts of the flood plain, but these are so small and altered by nearby development that they do not give a true picture of the former grandeur of the flood-plain vegetation. The preservation of Stotts Island, a small and fragile ecosystem, is of the utmost importance.

UPLAND FORESTS

The pattern of the plant communities on the hills of the Tweed Valley is easier to piece together because more forest remains free of development, particularly at altitudes nearing 1000 metres. The distribution of these plant communities is dependent on a number of interconnected factors including altitude, aspect, soil type and the degree of natural disturbance by wind or, more importantly, by fire. Rainforest of one type or another predominates in more fertile locations, but is replaced by sclerophyll forests and even heath when conditions are drier and particularly when fire has been more frequent. The transition between rainforest and sclerophyll forests is an extremely interesting zone forming a mobile boundary between the two communities. Sclerophyll forest can quickly invade rainforest which is susceptible to disturbance, especially fire, but rainforest can slowly choke out sclerophyll forest given enough time (probably centuries).

RAINFORESTS

There is considerable variation in the rainforests on the hills in and around the Tweed Valley. The New South Wales Forestry Commission generally classifies the forests into four types, subtropical, warm temperate, cool temperate, and dry rainforests, depending on the particular mix of species. The diversity in these forests is not only caused by the considerable variation in altitude, aspect, and soil type, but is also the result of the varying combinations of equatorial species, with their origins in South-East Asia, and temperate species with strong affinities with the flora of New Zealand and South America. This overlapping of species makes the local rainforests unique internationally. Both groups of species tend to be present in all types of rainforests but the equatorial floras dominate the subtropical rainforests, whereas southern floras are dominant in the cool temperate and dry types of forest.

The subtropical rainforests are the most complex community in both structure and diversity of species. They were formerly located on the immensely fertile red soils on the Lismore basalts and similar rock types. Unfortunately much of this land was highly desired by the pioneering settlers and little of the 'Big Scrub' remains today. Perhaps the last remaining examples of this type of rainforest have been preserved in the Big Scrub Flora Reserve on the southern foothills of the Nightcap Range, and in sheltered locations on the more fertile soils derived from gabbro on Mt Warning.

White booyong trees dominate this community but

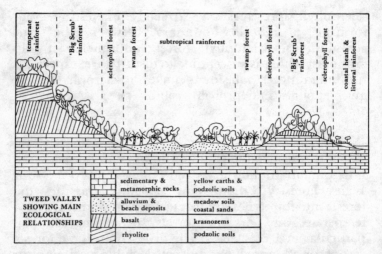

Fig. 11 Simplified cross-section of the valley showing the
main relationships between geology and vegetation

it is associated with many other tree species including
the Moreton Bay fig, strangler fig, rose marara, tamarind,
the striking flame tree and the majestic red cedar. Giant
stinging trees are also present particularly in disturbed
areas. These stinging trees can be easily recognised by
the large heart-shaped leaves which are often converted
into an intricate lace by a very hardy insect. Each leaf
of the giant stinger has poisonous hairs which will inflict
a painful sting on human beings and have been reported
to cause horses to become frenzied.

Many of these trees have flared root systems known
as 'buttress roots', that can begin many metres above
the ground. Scientists are divided as to the purpose of
these roots. Do they help support these huge trees ? Do
they help the tree gain nutrients by tapping supplies
of water near the surface of the soil, or do they assist
the tree in breathing by increasing the surface area of
the bark? Is it possible the buttresses do all three? The
early timber-cutters avoided the buttresses by using
planks called 'springboards', to get above the roots, in

the process avoiding any rotten wood that may exist in the 'pipe' of the tree. The springboard marks can be seen on the larger stumps still present in the forest, mute testaments to a bygone age.

Rainforests are more than trees as many other plants complete the diversity of this ecosystem. Epiphytes, plants that attach themselves to trees but do not live off them, such as birds nest ferns, staghorns, elkhorns and a large variety of beautiful orchids, add considerable beauty to these forests. The epiphytes solve the problem of rising above the canopy to the sunlight by attaching themselves to a tree growing skywards. This saves a considerable amount of energy and growth but they have to scavenge their food from the leaf and twig litter falling from the branches above. As well they have to have structures that can collect rainwater as it runs down the trunk since they have no roots to act as pipelines to the moisture in the soil below.

Strangler figs are one of the most interesting trees in the forests. They begin life as an epiphyte high in the canopy where their seeds coated with fertiliser have been dropped by a bird. The strangler fig's roots thread their way rapidly down the trunk to the ground and as they grow, they appear to 'strangle' their host tree. This is not actually the case in most instances, as the host tree often dies from natural causes long before it is 'strangled'. When the trunk of the host tree rots away a large hollow is left between the roots of the fig creating an impressive cathedral-like chamber. By this means the strangler fig grows faster than its rivals on the forest floor, many of which are still struggling for survival, patiently waiting for an opening to appear to give them the necessary light to reach the canopy.

Many types of palm are also present and they come in a large variety of sizes, often dominating areas of poor drainage or areas disturbed in the past by wind or fires. The relatively tall bangalow palm forms a lower storey in the canopy and its fruit is an important form of food for many fruitivorous birds. The midginbil or walking stick palm grows only to a few metres in height, but is prized as a walking stick. When the midginbil is cut below the root level and the roots are carved into a knob a light and highly decorative walking stick is produced. The flesh on the ripe berries can be chewed as a source of moisture and nourishment when you come across them, but they will hardly dent your hunger.

The most interesting palm of all resembles a vine, and is known locally as the 'lawyer vine' or 'wait-a-while'. Wait-a whiles have a long smooth cane in the older parts of the plant, but the business end is very prickly with long grasping barbed tendrils. You certainly have to 'wait-a-while' when they get hold of you and it can take some time to disentangle yourself from their lawyer-like grasp. The cane from the lawyer vine is used for basket-weaving, since it is thin and very flexible.

Among the many vines in the rainforests are the rope-like water vines clinging to the trees in a tangled and jumbled mass. It is thought that many of these vines are older than their host trees. When the host tree blows over, a common form of death in rainforests, the water vines climb other trees in order to reach the canopy again. This may explain the impossible tangle that some of these vines present.

Rainforest has a closed canopy allowing little direct sunlight to reach the forest floor. This excludes grasses, leaving the ground relatively free of undergrowth, except for shade-tolerant plants. Many ferns, some small and delicate, some attached to trees, and some tree ferns several metres tall compete with rainforest seedlings and some unusual lilies. The large Northern Gymea lily is found growing at its northernmost limit. The smaller cunjevoi lily, sometimes known as elephant ears, has medicinal properties and can be used as an antidote for the sting of the giant or Queensland stinging tree. Bush folklore has it that the cunjevoi is always found growing near the stingers. Small seedlings of rainforest trees complete the forest-floor community. The seedlings remain virtually dormant until there is a break in the canopy allowing sunlight to reach them and make possible their growth up into the canopy. Often these seedlings are very old plants awaiting an opening in the canopy, their internal mechanisms slowed down and adapted to their light-deprived conditions.

Rainforests lose much of their diversity as conditions that favour their growth deteriorate. In cooler or drier locations the forests become simpler and the diversity of species decreases. Many of the fascinating features of subtropical rainforest such as buttress roots and huge vines become less conspicuous as trees from southern floras become more dominant. Coachwood, a highly valued timber for aircraft construction in World War II, becomes dominant in drier locations but perhaps the most remarkable trees of the higher forests are the ancient Antarctic beeches.

In the cool temperate rainforests of the higher points on the plateaux, the Antarctic beeches are growing at their most northern limit and are a relict of former cooler climatic conditions. Under the stress of this marginal location the trees do not reproduce by seeds but by 'coppicing', the production of new stems from the existing root stock. Some botanists believe that they are too far north to reproduce by normal means but there is a possibility that coppicing is a method of regeneration adapted to conditions underneath a closed canopy. On the Bar Mountain where logging disturbed the canopy during the 1970s some reproduction by seedlings may have occurred in areas opened up to sunlight. A typical Antarctic beech tree is a circular arrangement of large gnarled trunks growing out from a mass of roots that can be as high as several metres above the ground. Some say that the height of this root system represents the quantity of soil lost through erosion during the many centuries that these trees have been growing.

Rainforest litter decomposes rapidly under the damp

conditions prevailing on the forest floor. The rotting of this litter into humus is assisted by many decomposing organisms including various types of moulds and fungi. Many of these are brightly coloured and some are even luminous at night. Rainforests recycle nutrients very efficiently, with most nutrients stored in the canopy and on or near the top layer of the soil. This is one of the reasons that rainforest trees have shallow root systems. The damp conditions and rapid rotting of litter means that the trees have to be quick to take up nutrients before they are washed out of the system and out of reach of the trees' roots. Additionally these conditions leave little fuel for ground fires making the rainforests 'fireproof'. However they can be burnt, particularly in periods of drought. Bushfires destroy rainforest and regeneration can take hundreds of years.

SCLEROPHYLL FORESTS (now called Open Forests)

The drier and less fertile areas of the Tweed were dominated by wet and dry sclerophyll forests. Sclerophyll trees have considerable resistance to drought and fires. Most common among the sclerophyll trees are the eucalypts and the wattles, but there are many others. The tough leaves covered with a waxlike outer layer are an adaptation to drought in that they reduce water loss through transpiration. However the protective coat lasts after the leaf has fallen and slows down the rate of decay of litter on the forest floor. Over a period of time quite large amounts of fuel may accumulate, creating ideal conditions for severe ground fires.

Ground fires eliminate competition from sensitive rainforest species, open up the forest floor to sunlight and in some species are necessary to open the hard seedpods and release the seeds. Most eucalypts recover easily from quite severe ground fires, even to the extent of having dormant buds beneath the surface bark ready to burst through and continue the vital process of transpiration. The fires favour sclerophyll trees and the trees almost seem to recognise this and produce the conditions that promote fires.

Wet Sclerophyll Forests (Tall Open Forests)

Sclerophyll forests do not have the closed canopy of rainforests and some direct sunlight reaches the ground. In wet sclerophyll forests the amount of direct sunlight reaching the forest floor is limited. Sclerophyll forests are dominated in this area by brush box (which is not a eucalypt), flooded gum, tallow wood, blue gum, forest oak, turpentine, and New England blackbutts (at altitudes over 600m.). The understorey often comprises rainforest species, broad-leafed shrubs and ferns, but insufficient light excludes grasses. Forests such as these have been an important source of hardwoods for the timber industry up to the late 1970s but were unfortunately logged too heavily. Little commercially valuable timber is currently available as the areas have been logged in the 1980s beyond what is now considered to be a sustained yield.

Dry Sclerophyll Forests (Open Forests)

In drier locations or where fires have been more frequent and severe, a drier type of sclerophyll forest exists. These locations are often on north facing slopes particularly those with the poorer rhyolite and sedimentary associated soils. Dry sclerophyll forests have a more open canopy and a lot of direct sunlight is available at ground level. White mahogany, pink bloodwood, grey ironbarks, and grey gums are among the main species of trees, often with an understorey of grasstrees (blackboys), blady grass, and kangaroo grass.

Heath

In extremely dry and exposed areas with thin soils heath types of vegetation are often found. Lemon and yellow tea-trees, bottle brushes, and grasstrees are the most common understorey plants. Heath is mainly found on isolated, steep peaks and ridge tops such as Mt Warning, Mt Wagawn, and the Tweed Pinnacle, or on the very thin and infertile soils derived from rhyolites at Daves Creek and the Doon Doon Saddle.

BOUNDARIES

The rainforest/sclerophyll forest boundary is an extremely interesting zone. Most rainforest species are hypersensitive to fire, and often completely destroyed by it. Their regeneration is prevented by the increased exposure to sunlight and resulting drier conditions but this is only a temporary situation. Wild fires convert rainforest areas into sclerophyll forests as eucalypts, wattles and associated species are favoured by the harsher conditions. The development of mature sclerophyll forest recreates the conditions necessary for the successful regeneration of a rainforest understorey. Repeated fires keep this understorey under control but if fire does not occur for a long period of time the understorey can gradually develop a complete or closed canopy preventing the regeneration of the sclerophyll species. In time the mature sclerophyll trees die out and the succession to rainforest is complete. The longest living species of the sclerophyll forests, the brush box and New England blackbutts, are therefore often found as emergent relics in the transition zone between sclerophyll and rainforests. As these trees can live for 400 years or more, the time period for the regeneration of rainforests must be very long indeed.

It is now widely accepted that the Australian Aboriginal people were skilful users of fire to control their environment. It is highly likely that the boundaries between rainforest and sclerophyll forest were in balance with the fire regime practised by the Aborigines, however the Aboriginal people ceased to be the dominant human influence in the Tweed Region by about 1870 and a new fire regime was introduced by the Europeans.

We have yet to learn how to use fire as a tool of environmental management, with the skill of the Aboriginal people. Modern fires tend to be less frequent but more severe and more likely to get out of control. The influence of wild fires on the boundary between these forests is uncertain as insufficient time has elapsed for the plant communities to strike a new balance with the conditions imposed by Europeans. The new fire regime is not the only new condition imposed on the local ecosystems as clear felling, selective logging, and a multitude of alien plants or weeds also complicate the total picture.

It is clear that the vegetation pattern in the Tweed is very complex, dynamic, and not yet fully understood by scientists. The basic ideas expressed above give a general outline of the vegetation pattern of the Tweed. The authors have not attempted to give a scientific dissertation on the botany of the area, partly because it would be out of place in a book such as this, but mainly because of their belief in the need for generalists. The specialists are uncovering vast amounts of specific information about particular items within our forests, but the Earth is not made in discrete bundles and the measure of our knowledge of this small part of Earth must inevitably be how well we understand how it all fits together.

FAUNA

The great diversity of plant communities within the caldera and on the rim, provides a wide variety of habitats for animal life, one of the reasons that this area has the richest fauna in Australia. The other main reason for the large number of different species present in the area, is that like the plant communities, the Tweed Region lies within the transition zone for tropical or

Torresian fauna and southern or Bassian species. Less is known about the animal life of the region than the plant life, as a lot of research remains to be done. The following account is a brief introduction to the fauna of the region, emphasising species that are most likely to be encountered by the bushwalker.

Birds

The bird life in the region is extremely diverse with over one-quarter of all the known bird species in Australia represented. The late Milton Trudgeon of Lismore, highly regarded as the local authority on bird life, recorded 207 separate species, including several migratory birds that pass through. Birds are often difficult to see in forests, particularly rainforests, but their presence is made clear by their noisy calls. Perhaps the most spectacular is the sharp call of the extremely shy whipbird. You will be very lucky if you see a whipbird, but their unmistakable calls are often heard in the rainforest.

Pigeon calls are also frequently heard as many species, including the endangered wompoo and red-crowned pigeons, feed on brightly coloured fruits of the rainforest trees. Many birds feed on the fruits of bangalow palm, fig, lilly pilly, and other fruit-bearing trees. They migrate from tree to tree seasonally as the fruits of each species ripen at different times of the year. They also migrate up-slope as the fruit of each tree ripen later in the cooler conditions at higher altitudes. There is a delay of approximately four days for each 100m of altitude so the fruiting of one species can last for a period of up to two months on the mountains. For this reason alone the preservation of the few remaining stands of rainforest at low altitudes is imperative.

You are more likely to see birds on the ground. The largest that you are likely to encounter is the scrub or brush turkey, a large black fowl with a red and yellow head. This bird scratches up huge mounds of litter to incubate its eggs, feeds on the ground and occasionally climbs trees for safety, but has clumsy flight. Some have become very tame now that most of the shooting has stopped, so they are often seen where tourists frequently have lunch, feeding on scraps thrown to them. One morning, in a remote section of the Lamington Plateau, one wandered through our camp site, but it rapidly disappeared when we climbed out of our sleeping bags to photograph it. You will have to be extremely fortunate, or need to spend a lot of time in the bush, to see the endangered Albert lyrebird and the rufous scrub-bird. There are many more birds in the sclerophyll forests but they are too numerous to list in this brief account. Studies quoted in the Mt Warning National Park plan of management have shown 177 bird species in the Border Ranges forests.

Mammals

A number of mammals inhabit this area, but are rarely seen during the day. You are more likely to see them during the early morning or late afternoon. Spot-lighting with a strong torch at night can be rewarding as many mammals are more easily found at this, their watering and feeding time. A number of possums inhabit the forests. These include the mountain, short-eared and ringtail varieties. Several small but interesting gliders live in the trees. The sugar, squirrel, pigmy and greater gliders have all been recorded in the Mt Warning State Park. Koalas are present in the sclerophyll forests on drier northern slopes of Mt Warning.

Ground-dwelling mammals are relatively rare in the forest, but are plentiful in the grassy edges of the forest. Bandicoots and pademelons announce their presence by the holes they dig in the forest soil as they search for food. The pademelons at the Binna Burra Camping Ground have become quite tame and can be approached at close quarters. Wallabies are quite shy and are difficult to see, but you can sometimes hear them bounding through the scrub ahead of you as they carefully remain out of view. A friendly marsupial mouse once investigated our camp at Rat-a-tat and was apparently not frightened by our torch light inspection of its activities. Other mammals include the spotted tiger cat, echidna, flying foxes, and dingoes which can occasionally be heard howling in the scrub but they are rarely seen. Some mammals reach the known limits of their distribution in this region. For example the Border Ranges is the southernmost limit for the parma wallaby and the northernmost limit for the dusky marsupial mouse.

Other Animals

There are a number of reptiles in the region. They range from small skinks and shiny fat black land mullet to large goannas over one metre in length. Several snakes can be seen. The most frequently encountered is the large but non-venomous carpet snake. This attractively marked snake kills its prey by crushing it with strong coils of its body. After swallowing a large meal a carpet snake curls up and sleeps it off, often on the edge of a track where its presence can give an inattentive bushwalker quite a fright. Carpet snakes obviously have no fear of predators as they will sleep peacefully as you walk by, showing no sign that they are aware of your presence. There are several venomous snakes in the region but they are seldom seen, particularly in winter. These include black snakes and the aggressive rough scale snake. Most snakes are seen basking in the sun in the open or in rocky areas. As cold-blooded animals they absorb essential warmth from the environment. The best way to cope with snakes is to allow them time to sneak away as they are afraid of humans. Most people in Australia who get bitten by snakes, do so in an attempt to kill them. If you watch where you are walking and leave snakes alone, the chance of being bitten is extremely rare. Remember too that snakes are protected.

A detailed survey of amphibians is yet to be done in the area, but there are many interesting frogs, some rare and endangered and some yet to be discovered. The pouched frog, which rears its young in brood pouches, is kown to occur only in this region. Other interesting species include the giant barred river frog, and Loveridge's frog. The overlapping of northern and southern species has resulted in a species rich butterfly fauna including the Richmond River birdwing, the big greasy, capaneus butterfly, four-bar swordtail, pale green triangle and the regent skipper butterflies.

The creeks have a world of their own. The most likely species that you will encounter are the eels and fresh water lobsters or crays, particularly the Lamington blue crayfish which in wet weather is often encountered on the track well away from streams. The eel can be found, even in small streams high in the mountains. Sometimes very large eels can be seen in the larger swimming holes further downstream. They swim around leisurely without apparent fear almost as if they are daring you to enter their domain. Perhaps the most maligned form of wildlife, particularly by inexperienced walkers, is the bush leech. These relatively harmless creatures are sometimes thick on the ground, especially after rain, but they can easily be repelled by the use of a good insect repellent. They are so harmless that often you will not be aware of their presence and if you do notice them, they can easily be pulled off with your fingers. The best defence against leeches is to keep moving, keep rest stops to a minimum and don't make continual panic stops to check for them.

The study of wildlife can considerably enhance your enjoyment of walking in the bush, but you can't always rely on finding a particular species. Wildlife is often difficult to find but can be encountered when least expected. These chance observations can often be the most vividly remembered experience of the trip. It is of the utmost importance that the rich wildlife of the region is preserved so that future generations may enjoy worthwhile experiences when walking in this area. The maintenance of a diverse range of habitats and the protection of animal species from disruption caused by human activities is vital to the survival of viable populations of this fauna.

PART II
BUSHWALKS

4
Walks inside the caldera

The logical place to begin our series of bushwalks is with a leisurely stroll up Mt Warning. This remnant of one of the largest shield volcanoes to exist on Earth is the point of origin of the current spectacular landscapes and has nurtured many interesting flora and fauna types in the valley and its surrounds. Here details of walks found inside the walls of the caldera are given, and later chapters will deal with the caldera rim walks in an anti-clockwise progression.

Mt Warning

As this is composed of the materials that made up the former central core of the Tweed volcano, it makes an ideal point from which to begin a study of this unique region.

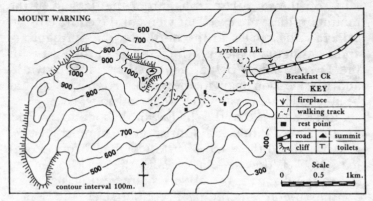

Fig. 12 The Mt Warning area (After the NSW Parks and Wildlife track map)

To reach Mt Warning drive to Murwillumbah, cross the bridge and continue on to the Uki signpost near the top of the hill. Follow this road through Bray Park to the Mt Warning turnoff, then follow the bitumen road to the picnic area at the base of the mountain. The road is well signposted and no difficulties should be experienced.

Walkers will need comfortable footwear, something to drink since water is not available on the track, and a raincoat and jumper as conditions can change quite rapidly on the mountain. The walk is 4.4 kilometres along well-constructed footpaths with a short scramble up a steep rock section at the end. Even the unfit can do this walk easily provided that they allow enough time. The recommended time allowance is about four hours for the return trip. The main danger for the ill-prepared is being caught out in the dark. The best time for the walk is winter or on an early morning after rain. At these times the air is clear and the views are superb.

The walk progresses upwards through subtropical rainforest, which gradually changes with altitude to heath. This change is mainly due to reduced temperatures, thinner soils, and the greater exposure to wind on the steeper sections. From the flat top of the mountain there are excellent views of the entire erosion caldera. The ranges to the north are the Springbrook and Lamington plateaux which merge in the west with the Tweed Range. Using the direction finder provided and the location map in the introduction you should be able to locate most of the inner caldera walks.

Stories have it that the shadow of the mountain picks out the Tweed Pinnacle at sunrise on the summer solstice, however the authors have yet to test that theory. Local man Noel Tetlow regularly walks the track to see the sun come up and has met all sorts of interesting characters on the summit, including a couple celebrating their engagement in full formal gear, tails, gown, chicken and champagne, carried to the top on sturdy and somewhat muddy bushwalking boots.

Unfortunately the intense use of this area has forced the National Parks and Wildlife to ban camping on the top and to ban fires as well. Leave earlier and carry a torch and a small stove or thermos and you can still enjoy the spectacle of the sun's fiery rise out of the Pacific. During 1988 work was carried out on the top of the mountain to provide better facilities. The work included platforms to protect the area from erosion, to raise walkers above the surrounding scrub and to prevent visitors from wandering over the precipitous drops

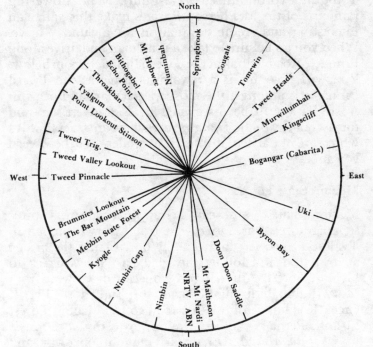

Fig. 13 The direction of points named in the text as seen from the top of Mt Warning. To use locate a known point and orient (Murwillumbah is a convenient point)

surrounding the summit. The picnic area at the base of the walk has toilets and cooking facilities (wood supplied) as well as pamphlets supplied by National Parks. While you are there, take the time to stroll across to Lyrebird Lookout (about 200m.) and if it is quiet listen to the profusion of bird life.

Tyalgum walks

The middle arm of the Tweed River has carved out a broadly dished valley to the northwest of Mt Warning. The valley is served by the picturesque village of Tyalgum (pronounced Tal-gum). The towering ramparts of the McPherson Ranges make this valley an interesting and scenic destination for a Sunday drive. When you go be sure to take a road map and drive along Pinnacle Road to look at the Tweed Pinnacle from below. You will find this is a rewarding drive as the Tweed Pinnacle is amongst the most spectacular landforms in Australia yet to be discovered by the advertisers and tourist bodies. In the Tyalgum area there are several walks which are of particular interest to students of the Tweed volcano.

Mebbin State Forest

Mebbin State Forest can be approached from three separate directions. Drive west from Murwillumbah to Tyalgum, turn left immediately on crossing the bridge at Tyalgum and follow the road past Brays Creek to Mebbin Forest. Alternatively you can drive west from Murwillumbah through Uki and turn right at the Byrrill Creek Road and follow this road to the Mebbin Forest turnoff. Perhaps the best way to go to this location is to take the round trip by driving out one way and returning the other. Mebbin Forest can also be entered from the Kyogle Road by taking the Hanging Rocks Road which turns off to the north from a signposted point west of the village of Kunghur. This road joins with Cadell Road in the forest. A four-wheel drive vehicle is not necessary in dry weather but is advisable when the forest roads are wet.

The timber-cutters' camp at Mebbin Forest has been converted into a camping and picnic area with pit toilets, cold showers, drinking water on tap, barbeque facilities, firewood, and garbage bins. Camp overnight at no cost, handfeed the butcher birds with meat, and explore the network of forestry roads. The well-maintained camp is located at the junction of Cadell and Cutters Camp roads. A short but rewarding walking trail leads from the camping ground down a steep bank to a small creek.

Although the bank is steep the track is graded, making it a pleasant stroll. This is an excellent place to study the transition from wet sclerophyll forest, growing on the upper slope of the bank, to rainforest growing on the flood plain below. Tall tallow wood, flooded gum, bloodwood, brush box and turpentine trees dominate the top of the track. The understorey has native ginger, a few palms, ferns and broad-leafed shrubs. Some scattered rainforest seedlings are present but, apart from the edge of the forest, no grass grows.

About halfway down the hill the sclerophyll trees are few, but large and rather old. A low but complete canopy of rainforest trees prevents the regeneration of eucalypt and associated species of trees. This is the transition zone between wet sclerophyll forest and rainforest. Many other rainforest plants grow in this area. There are midginbil palms, wait-a-whiles and epiphytes as well as some vines. Towards the bottom of the slope the relict sclerophyll trees disappear and true rainforest is reached.

The restricted flood plain between the bottom of the slope and the creek has a small but fascinating subtropical rainforest. There are many bangalow palms, water vines, epiphytes and all of the features that make rainforests so interesting. Perhaps the most spectacular feature of this forest is the large strangler figs. Three, in particular, are as magnificent as you will see anywhere.

If you have the time trace out the roots of these immense trees as they search for nutrients and water. You will be amazed at the length and dimensions of the roots. It is almost as if the trees have their own private pipelines to pump water out of the creek.

The track ends at a small pool in the creek. The pool is too small and shallow for swimming, but it is a pleasant place to cool off on a hot day. This is a very easy and accessible walk, and is particularly recommended to those with a special interest in rainforest who are not prepared to undertake strenuous walks in less accessible areas. It is an excellent place to take young children.

The giant ironbark tree

While at Mebbin Forest you should take a look at the giant ironbark tree. Proceed southwest along Cadell Road for approximately 1.5 kilometres then turn left into Lemon Tree Road. This is a dry-weather road only and should not be attempted in a conventional vehicle if the road surface is wet. Approximately 2.5 kilometres along Lemon Tree Road a signpost on the left marks the beginning of the walk down to the giant ironbark tree. The walk is extremely short (50m. or less) and leads to a magnificent grey ironbark tree. The Forestry Commission saved the tree from the axe as one example of the magnificent trees in this forest before logging. The exceptional girth of the tree (over 6 m.) is matched by an impressive straight trunk that soars more than 50 metres with elegance and grace. The area around the tree has been fenced off to prevent damage by the compacting effect of tourists' feet on the soil. A local forestry officer, Ranger Cadell, loved the forest and this particular tree so much that he had his ashes distributed around its base.

Brummies Lookout

Brummies Lookout is a high point on the western section

of the ring dyke surrounding Mt Warning. The lookout is very near the boundary between Wollumbin State Forest and Mt Warning National Park. Just before you cross the bridge on the way into Tyalgum from Murwillumbah, take the left turn up the Tyalgum Ridge Road. The road is signposted '4 Wheel Drive–Dry Weather Only' but can be negotiated with care in a conventional vehicle if the road surface is dry. Proceed along this road until you reach the junction of Brummies Road and Condowie Road, the road surface is usually good to this point. Take Brummies Road veering to the right but proceed with caution as the road receives little traffic. The walking track to Brummies Lookout is signposted and is just before the end of the road, but you will need to go to the end to turn around.

The walk to the lookout is only 500 metres long and although it is all uphill it is not too strenuous. When you leave your car you will be in wet sclerophyll forest and gradually climb into rainforest on the rich soils derived from syenite, a type of intrusive igneous rock. The steepness of the terrain causes the soils to be thin and rocky, and as a result the rainforest trees are rather small. The stumps of trees logged in the past along the lower section of the track are evidence of the tenacity of timber-workers in the past. Towards the top the trees are festooned with moss from the cloud and mist, frequent at this altitude. Just before the summit there is an abrupt change from rainforest to kangaroo grass and grasstree heath.

The summit of Brummies is flat and fairly large and there are good views in all directions if you are prepared to walk around. The best views are towards Mt Warning with the rainforest below you in Cedar Creek which runs south between the ring dyke and the mountain. Away to the south you can see Mt Uki and the Sisters on the southern part of the ring dyke.

Brummies has been an important lookout ever since the first white settlers entered the district. Legend has it that Brummie was a cedar-getter who used the peak to spot valuable cedar trees during spring when the pink new foliage made them distinctive in the forest canopy.

Cedar Creek

Cedar Creek is a small tributary of Byrrill Creek that drains the valley between the southwestern quarter of the ring dyke and Mt Warning. This is a wilderness area in Mt Warning National Park that has no graded tracks or walking trails. It should only be attempted by walkers who have had previous experience in travelling through wilderness areas, or parties that have a guide familiar with this locality.

It is best to start the walk from Brummies Road in Wollumbin State Forest 100 metres or so before the walk to Brummies Lookout. It is recommended that you walk to the top of Brummies Lookout before commencing this walk as the magnificent view of Cedar Creek will give you an appreciation of the wilderness you are about to experience. Proceed east from Brummies Road down the extremely steep slope clad with rainforest on fertile soils weathered from gabbro, to the creek below. The steepness of this slope is the reason for recommending the walk in this direction. The walk can be completed by rock-hopping down the creek until you come to private land and can reach the Cedar Creek Road. You may experience some difficulty with lantana thickets at the edge of the park. On some occasions magnificent fresh-water lobsters or Lamington blue crays can be seen near the creek especially after rain when the higher water level in the creek appears to drive them out. Even though the creek is small surprisingly large eels can be seen in it, but they are very shy and can hide so effectively that they seem to vanish.

An easier alternate route, for those who can find it, is to walk towards an old miners' track, but be warned it is difficult to find unknown tracks in a wilderness area. After descending to Cedar Creek from Brummies

Road proceed down Cedar Creek for several hundred metres until you come to a tributary gully entering from the left over a spectacular slab of rock. Walk up this gully for several metres and then veer to the right out of the gully and cross over the low divide between Cedar Creek and one of its tributaries, Pretty Creek. Notice how the vegetation differs on the slopes of this divide. The shaded southern side, facing Cedar Creek, is covered with a rainforest of small trees and lawyer vines while the sunny northern side, facing Pretty Creek, is more open and has a large magnificent flooded gum tree.

Follow Pretty Creek downstream for several hundred metres until you can see several strangler fig trees on the left-hand slope. These are quite difficult to find if you are not familiar with the area. Walk up past these trees and veer slightly to your right and find some large boulders on top of the ridge. These boulders were used in the past as a shelter for shooters seeking pigeons and scrub turkeys. Even though you are in a wilderness area you can still see the ubiquitous empty tinny that unfortunately litters much of the Australian bush. The old miners' track is approximately 30 metres past the large rocks. Follow this track to the right until it links up with an old four-wheel drive road, then follow this road to the left until it joins Cedar Creek Road.

If you can't find any of these landmarks you can always follow Pretty Creek downstream until it joins Cedar Creek and rock-hop down the creek until you can gain access to the road. It is possible to explore this area from both ends until you become familiar with the lay of the land but it must be stressed that you should not attempt this walk unless you are sufficiently experienced to cope with trackless areas.

Amaroo walk

Amaroo walk has been constructed by the Forestry Commission in an area selectively logged in the past. It consists of old snigging trails and forestry roads that are no longer required and have been converted to a walking trail. Amaroo walk once connected North Wollumbin Road and Brummies Road but the track has fallen into such disrepair at the North Wollumbin Road end that the through walk is almost impossible. The Forestry Commission is considering making this into a loop walk by closing off the northern end. The closure has been effected by natural re-growth but as yet there is no sign of a loop being constructed.

Even though this area has been selectively logged in the past it is worth visiting. There is still a rainforest canopy and the walker may not realise that this area has previously been harvested. The expert will recognise the previous disturbance as large and spectacular trees are missing. About 400 metres in from the beginning of the walk look out for a large rosewood. The tree is imposing and one of the largest of its species you will find. The rosewood is about 15 metres uphill from the track and can easily be seen and approached from the track. The distinctive flaky bark and its large girth (approximately 5 metres) will help you identify the correct tree. This walk may be attempted by itself as it only requires approximately one hour, is comparatively flat, and can be sensibly combined with Brummies Lookout. The experienced and adventurous may wish to combine these two with Cedar Creek. The combined walks will take approximately seven hours and transport will have to be arranged for you at both ends.

Stotts Island

Stotts Island, located next to the highway between Chinderah and Tumbulgum, has the only remaining examples of flood plain vegetation on the Tweed (see Fig. 10), and has been dedicated as a flora reserve mainly for scientific purposes. The remains of a small walking trail previously constructed on part of the island can be followed by interested walkers, but access to the island is only possible by boat.

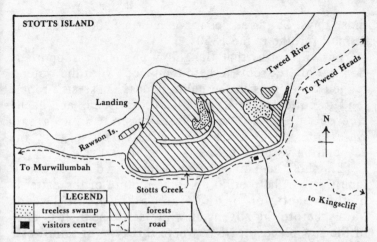

Fig. 14 Stotts Island is located alongside the highway about halfway between Tumbulgum and Chinderah

The old circular walking track commences near the remains of the wharf located on the north-western corner of the island. The track passes through the fringing rainforest on the natural levee into the palm glades that dominate the centre of the island. Many trees were named to assist those interested in studying the vegetation and some of the signs may still be seen.

A short track leads off the circular track, where it reaches the river bank. This track leads downstream through the fringing forest to two spectacular fig trees. It is possible to walk through the roots of one of the trees and the other has a most impressive set of buttressed roots. If you continue from these figs into the nearby palm glade you will pass by some majestic hoop pines. Hoop pines tend to grow in the transition zone between the palm glades and the rainforest. Hoop pines were sought after by the early cedar-cutters and many were floated downstream and loaded onto sailing ships, but history makes little mention of them as their value was rather ordinary compared to the extremely valuable red cedar. A hoop pine was worth about $20 which was a large sum in those days, but a red cedar was worth $200 which was a small fortune in the 1850s.

You will notice that Bangalow palms are supported on a set of stilt roots to help them cope with the water-logged conditions in the palm glades. These stilt roots tend to collect debris and silt during floods and each tree occupies its own separate mound. Some giant water gums (which are not a eucalypt) also grow in association with the palms.

This short acquaintance with these two forest communities will help build up some picture of the pattern of the vegetation on the flood plain of the Tweed Valley before the advent of white settlement. It is one of the few places in NSW where this type of rainforest can be viewed in what is basically its natural state.

A picnic table and barbecue formerly existed at the wharf, haunted by a large goanna which, attracted by the smell of cooking meat, occasionally invited itself to dinner. Visitors are also advised to use an insect repellent as protection against mosquitoes. It must be stressed that Stotts Island, because it is so small, is an extremely fragile area and it is imperative that visitors take great care not to cause any damage to its ecology.

While visiting Stotts Island you should look at the area being restored to rainforest between Stotts Creek and the highway. Look for the Visitors Centre just past the western end of the double lanes called Oak Avenue. From the carpark at the Visitors' Centre you can stroll through the area being restored. Bruce Chick , a local identity, has planted hundreds of local rainforest trees along the creek bank to restore this important area to something like its former grandeur. Bruce has planted thousands of trees in the Tweed Valley: Murwillumbah High School grounds and the Murwillumbah Golf Club fairways are other monuments to his work. He has also become somewhat of an expert on the propagation of rainforest species and leads groups of interested persons off into the forest to pass on his vast knowledge and enthusiasm for rainforest trees.

Another interesting activity for the fit and well-equipped is to circumnavigate the island by canoe or small boat. This will give some idea of the size of the island and a glimpse of the other plant communities found there. Stotts Creek, the channel between the island and the Pacific Highway was cleared in the past to allow cane barges to collect sugar cane from the nearby farms when water transport was the main means of collecting cane for milling. This disturbance has allowed weeds to infest the river bank, but natural regeneration of the mangroves is slowly restoring the area.

The mangroves now block the channel to large boats but make the trip by small boat more interesting. A section of treeless swamp can be seen from the main channel shortly after rounding the long narrow spit on the eastern end of the island. This area is very low and high water levels and regular inundation with brackish water preclude tree growth. Two other small islands are also found in this part of the river but neither of these yet support a rainforest community. Given the right conditions they may grow to something the size of Stotts Island and develop their own distinctive communities in much the same way as the main island has developed.

Stotts Island is moving downstream in a kind of rolling action as the river removes material from its exposed upstream edge and deposits silt downstream in the lee of the island. The island itself has a kind of bowl-shape as the most active area of deposition by the stream is around its edges. The centre of the island is low lying and swampy. It is reputed to be a floating island and while this may be true of some of the vegetation in the inner swamps the island itself is firmly grounded as any inspection of the exposed banks will confirm. However erosion and deposition are steadily moving the material in its northern edge downstream and thus moving the whole island downstream like a giant whale being pushed out to sea.

Hellhole Falls

WARNING: THIS TRIP MAY REQUIRE A FOUR WHEEL DRIVE VEHICLE. CONVENTIONAL VEHICLES SHOULD ONLY ATTEMPT THE TRIP IF THE ROADS ARE DRY.

This walk is a short but interesting stroll into the southern section of the ancient Chillingham volcanics. These old rhyolites and tuffs were laid down long before Mount Warning erupted through the centre of their narrow north-south band. The Chillingham Volcanics are well known for their semi-precious stones and rock oddities such as thunder eggs, but here a creek has cut a magnificent set of waterfalls into the ancient rhyolites. The rhyolites are clearly flow banded and the banding exposes the tortuous twists and folds in the slow moving lava as it was extruded and rapidly cooled.

Take the Uki road from Murwillumbah, at the memorial in Uki take the left hand turn to Rolands Creek. This road becomes Manns Road and continues all the way to Mullumbimby but about halfway there you take Middle Ridge Road and follow it until you come to Sand Ridge Road, this will turn off to your left and winds its way steeply down to an old pile bridge. Stop at the bridge and walk down the creek to your right. The distance is only a hundred metres or so and the walking relatively easy. The creek drops off in a series of rapids and small falls with lovely potholes until it finally plunges over two spectacular falls. Getting to the bottom of the falls would require a full days expedition through steep and difficult country but the view from the top is magnificent. Take your swimmers for a refreshing dip in one of the lovely plunge pools under the smaller falls.

The whole trip will take an hour or more but it is well worth the effort, the contortions in the rocks are spectacular, the views magnificent, and you can easily continue down over the divide to Mullumbimby through some of the pretty valleys cut into the southern remnants of the Volcano.

5
Numinbah—Springbrook walks

The first of the plateau remnants of the old volcano begins in the hills above Tweed Heads. The McPhersons gradually rise from Point Danger through the Tomewin area until they reach the soaring cliffs of the Springbrook Plateau. Further west the Springbrook area has been separated from the Lamington by the great slash of the Numinbah Valley, a remnant of one of the larger radial streams whose headwaters have been pirated by the Tweed. The approach to the Springbrook Plateau takes you through the Numinbah Valley and this is the order in which the walks are treated.

The Cougals

The first major peaks encountered on the northern side of the erosion caldera are the Cougals. The twin peaks of the Cougals are located along the Tomewin Road. From Murwillumbah cross the bridge, turn right then left, then follow the main street to the left turn into Queensland Road, at the foot of the hill. From there follow the signposts up to Tomewin. When you have almost reached the top of the range take the turn to the Garden of Eden. Follow this road until you reach a gate in the tick fence. Leave your car there, climb the fence and follow the fence to the west. Apart from an early steep climb, the going is easy until you reach the base of the East Cougal. Contour around to the right for about 50 metres and you will be confronted by a sharp scramble up a steep rock section to the top.

From the top there are excellent views of the Tweed Valley and the ranges leading down to the coast. Westward the ranges rise in the second spectacular peak, then continue on to the bulk of the Springbrook Plateau. In September a pair of binoculars will reveal vast sprays of rock orchids on the northern face of the West Cougal.

Views away to the north cover Boyds Butte and the upper regions of the Currumbin Valley.

When retracing your steps have a look at the cave which penetrates right through the peak. The track goes up from the near vicinity of the tick fence. If you wish you can continue on to the West Cougal. Our information suggests that this walk is rather difficult and the views are not as good. As we have not walked this section we do not recommend that you attempt it unless you are an experienced walker with a good head for heights.

The Cougals walk is a pleasant stroll and should take about four hours. The walking is not very strenuous and the views are amply rewarding. Take drinking water with you as there is no water source available on the walk.

Tomewin Rocks

While in the area walkers may wish to take another short walk, this time through an area of highland forest. Go to the Tomewin tick gates, park in the vicinity of the gates, and this time walk east along the fence. This track will eventually take you to Tweed Heads but less than an hour's walk out from the gate you will come across a large rock with some restricted views across the eastern part of the valley. The walk is easy and quite enjoyable with some good forest stands. The rocks are composed of agglomerate or breccia, a type of rock formed by the mixture of volcanic bombs and ash blown out during one of the explosive phases of the eruption.

Numinbah Valley

The Numinbah Valley is one of the remains of the large radial streams flowing off the old shield. The Tweed River cut back its valley faster and 'pirated' Numinbah Creek's headwaters leaving a large valley occupied by a very small stream. The deep slash of the valley has created spectacular landforms and has cut down through the layers of the shield exposing them to view. Many interesting walks are found in the valley both for scenic beauty and study.

The Numinbah Valley may be reached from either the Gold Coast via Advancetown or the Tweed via Crystal Creek and Chillingham. East of the valley is the Springbrook Plateau, while on the west is the Lamington, specifically Daves Creek and the Shipstern Range.

Natural Bridge

The turnoff to the Natural Bridge is only a few kilometres past the Numinbah tick gate when approaching from the Tweed, and is well signposted. From the well-appointed carpark a short circuit walk takes you down under the bridge, and returns over the bridge. The walk is not strenuous and at a leisurely pace will take little more than an hour.

The bridge has been formed at the edge of a lava flow. As it plunges over the edge of the flow the stream has undercut the flow, creating a large cavern. Later the stream has potholed its way down through the lava flow leaving a section of the flow behind as a natural arch. The main elements of the developmental process are well documented in a self-guiding walk brochure available at the park entrance. Adventurous souls have been known to dive from the arch into the deep plunge pool below the falls. The National Parks do not approve of this practice as there is great danger if debris has been swept into the pool by floods. If you have your swimming costume and are prepared to brave the cold water (even in summer) you can swim out under the falls.

In the cavern you can look up and see the underside of a lava flow. The lumpy nature of the roof could well be a form of pillow lava. Pillow lavas are formed when the lava is extruded onto a wet surface so if these are pillow lavas there are interesting geological conclusions to be drawn. Either we had a lake-dammed stream occupying much the same area as the current stream or the lava was extruded onto a surface soil that was very wet. This is perhaps similar to the hanging swamps found in the Gibraltar Range National Park west of Grafton. The weaker material between the pillows may well have been ash or sediments over which the lava was extruded. At one point you can see a place where seepage through the rock is occurring and from the top you can see the corresponding large pothole which is in the process of being drilled down through the lava flow. This illustrates graphically the manner in which the bridge was created.

Look in the darker section over near the falls and you may well see the glowing filaments of glow-worms. These glow-worms are not really worms at all but the larvae of the mycetophilid fly, a fungus-gnat. On going back to the carpark look near the track intersection at the park entrance for the giant strangler fig. The host tree has completely rotted away, leaving the hollow lattice-work of the strangler. Many of the trees near the track entrance have been named. Some are easily recognised, such as the giant stinging tree, the hoop pine and the strangler fig, others are much less readily identifiable as is the case with most rainforest species.

Bushrangers Caves——Numinbah

From the Numinbah border gates an hour's walk up the tick fence to the west brings you to a most fascinating area. The walk is all in the open along a track kept cleared for the fence inspector's horse. This walk is one for an early morning, a cloudy day, or winter. Drinking water is usually available at the caves but the area has been well scavenged for firewood so take a small stove for a 'cuppa'.

On the NSW side follow the fence up to the cliff line. Climb over the fence and follow the well-trodden path around to the large overhang that is referred to as 'Bushrangers Caves'. The name is somewhat misleading as it is hard to imagine bushrangers hiding out in such a location. There would have been slim pickings for any such foolhardy desparadoes. At the top of the cliff line above there is a pile of slaty rocks supposedly the remains of their lookout post, but more likely an Aboriginal site if it has any significance at all.

Archaeological studies done by the University of Queensland have shown remains in the caves of Aboriginal cooking fires at least 5000 years old , so there is some possibility that this was a site of some significance to the local tribes. It may have been a point for ceremonial trading and communication between the tribes of the Tweed and the Nerang area, or a staging-point in journeys between the two districts.

The cliffs above the caves are of rhyolite, and the back of the cave is of tuff, similar to the cave at the Natural Bridge, where erosion has also exploited a weakness between two dissimilar rock types. These caves are at a much higher level which suggests that they are related to a later but similar phase of eruption to that which produced the Natural Bridge. In the roof of the cave you can see similar formations to the Natural Bridge, the rounded rocks which resemble pillow lavas, set in volcanic ash.

The dry dusty floor of the overhang makes a convenient camp site for an overnight stay and seepage pools at the back of the overhang provide drinking water. Seepage from the cliff above provides a shower in idyllic surrounds. It is not too far from the road and is surrounded by large trees giving an air of isolation and wilderness. Just before you enter the main overhang there is a large stone slab which has broken away from the cliff face. The adventurous can climb under this stone slab and emerge on the far side. A strangler fig has attached itself to the rock, sending its roots down to tap the moisture at the base of the cliffs.

Mt Wagawn

For the fit and adventurous the Bushrangers Caves are also the starting-point for a difficult but rewarding climb to the top of Mt Wagawn. Wagawn's views are the equal of any in the caldera, and from Wagawn easy walking along the National Parks track system will take you to Mt Hobwee, or through to Binna Burra, or even through to O'Reillys and points further west.

The Wagawn track continues past the caves along the base of the cliffs for about 200 metres. You come to a point where you can scramble up to the next cliff line. Go left at this cliff until you come to a scramble up to the next cliff, then left again until you find yourself on the edge of the scarp. From there it is straight up the middle of the ridge to the top. The track is well marked with tape and despite the steepness is not nearly as arduous as it looks from the road at the tick gates. The vegetation is interesting as it is forced to adapt to the very steep slopes between rhyolite flows and the exposed location out on the edge of the scarp.

Along the second cliff line you will notice the strong horizontal banding of the rocks. This slate-like rock is a flow-banded rhyolite. The rocks break into flat pieces with relatively sharp edges and with a little imagination the pile of rocks, which are the alleged bushrangers' hut, might be a debris heap left over from Aboriginal tool construction. The area is certainly worthy of more detailed analysis than it has currently been given. Following this cliff line along to the left will bring you to the spine of the ridge, which you then follow to the top. A last short scramble brings you out onto a narrow rock platform from which the views across the Tweed and down the Numinbah valleys are breathtaking. Mt Wagawn is the beginning of the National Parks graded walking tracks and you can continue on to Binna Burra or O'Reillys. Binna Burra is only two hours away and this route is an interesting and adventurous way to visit or leave the resort, provided you can suitably arrange your transport. The climb up to Mt Wagawn is very steep and should only be attempted by the fit and agile, but the rewards are definitely worth the effort. The less fit and agile should attempt the walk from the Binna Burra end.

The Bushrangers Caves walk can easily be done in a morning or an afternoon and is an ideal introduction to the bush and the volcano for children. Even very young children can do the walk with a minimum of assistance from adults. Apart from two fairly steep sections the walk is easy and even the unfit should be able to manage it provided that they set an appropriate pace.

Springbrook

Springbrook is the smallest and most accessible of the three plateaux of the scenic rim. It was extensively cleared by the pioneers and converted to dairy farms but most, not viable, have fallen into disuse or have been redeveloped. Some areas however have not been cleared but these are mainly at high altitudes or on and below the scarps. These areas have been proclaimed national parks and are of interest to the bushwalker.

It is impossible to get the true sense of wilderness on Springbrook because it is too closely settled but there are advantages in visiting this plateau. Springbrook is the ideal place for the inexperienced to begin bushwalking because of its accessibility and its facilities. All of the roads are sealed and shops and other tourist enterprises are located nearby. The walks are relatively easy, short and well developed and National Parks provide a comprehensive and well-presented track map.

Springbrook can be reached by road from either the Gold Coast City via Mudgeeraba or from Murwillumbah via the Numinbah Valley. Camp in the well-appointed camping ground above Purlingbrook Falls in Gwongorella National Park at the end of Forestry Road.

This ground is attractively landscaped and equipped with septic toilets, tank water, barbeque and picnic facilities, and firewood. One of the special features of this camping ground is the bird life, especially in the morning when their delightful chorus will act as your alarm clock.

Purlingbrook Falls

There are many interesting waterfalls on Springbrook but Purlingbrook Falls are undoubtedly the most spectacular. Springbrook, an upper tributary of the west branch of Little Nerang Creek, plunges 130 metres over the massive rhyolite lava flows that form the cliff line almost completely surrounding the plateau. Lookouts above both the eastern and western sides of this fall give spectacular views of it and the valley below. A 4-kilometre circular walking track, the 'Falls Circuit', includes both of these lookouts and a spectacular view from beneath the falls as the track passes below and behind these falls. Hand rails and steps assist and protect the walker on difficult terrain and adequate signs ensure that you don't get lost.

Take the track in the recommended clockwise direction. The vegetation on top of the plateau above the falls is sclerophyll forest growing on poor soil weathered from rhyolite with brush box, gums, tallow wood and turpentine trees. Large wattles and a heath-like understorey suggest frequent fires in the past. The track passes the Western Lookout and then proceeds to the top of the smaller Tanninaba Falls. This stream flows over the top of a rhyolite lava flow before plunging over the cliffs. After summer storms many shiny black land mullet sunbake on the track to dry out their skin. The track follows the top of the gorge before zig-zagging down the steep slope at the end of the cliff line. The vegetation changes to rainforest as you descend into the gorge, partly the result of increased shelter and moisture in the valley and partly because the stream has cut right through the poorer rhyolites and into the richer basalt lava flows below.

The track passes below the Tanninaba Falls. The interesting feature of these falls is that more water flows both over the top and downstream from the falls than can be observed falling down the cliff face. Most of the water flows in joint cracks in the rocks of the cliff face and is therefore out of sight. The track forks just before reaching the bottom of Purlingbrook Falls. The left junction takes you to the Warringa Swimming Pool approximately 1 kilometre down stream. This track is recommended if you wish to have a closer look at the rainforest and if you fancy a swim in a refreshing mountain stream. The right junction takes you under the falls and completes the circuit.

All of the large and spectacular waterfalls are on the radial streams that flow away from the Tweed Valley and are the result of a more resistant band of rhyolite rocks that form the cliff lines surrounding the plateaux. Purlingbrook Falls have been created because the layer of rhyolite lavas has resisted erosion more successfully than the less resistant Lismore basalts below them. When viewed from the gorge the rhyolite lavas can clearly be seen as a massive layer overhanging slightly the softer basalts below. The falls have cut through several separate flows of basalt lavas and these form several narrow ledges between the overhanging rhyolites above and the plunge pool below. The walking track follows the widest of these ledges but the walker is protected by hand rails where this ledge is dangerously narrow. There is a spectacular view from behind the falling curtain of water from this section of the track and a magnificent rainbow can be seen rising from the plunge pool when the sun is at the right angle to the falls.

The track continues to the top of the falls in a similar manner to the track down, but the grade is slightly better and fewer steps have been constructed because the terrain is less difficult. The Eastern Lookout is located at the top of the falls and gives a good view of the stream plunging out into space from the top of a rhyolite lava flow. Finally the Springbrook is crossed by a small footbridge and the circuit is complete.

Best of all Lookout

The Best of all Lookout walk, situated on the edge of the caldera rim is located at the end of Repeater Station Road at the highest point on the plateau. Drive to the end of the road and park in a small parking area above the Repeater Station. A short walk of 400 metres takes you through temperate rainforest, festooned with moss, to the most accessible grove of Antarctic beech trees in the region, the most northerly and therefore marginal limit of their distribution. They are fantastically twisted and gnarled in shape, with a great deal of their root system above ground level. A fence protects these trees from the trampling effects of tourists' feet and a detailed sign provides information about this interesting species.

The Best of all Lookout is located at the end of the track 50 metres from the beech trees. A small wire-netting fence protects the viewer and allows even those with a poor head for heights to relax and enjoy the spectacular view of the eroded caldera, the Tweed Valley, below. A 180° panoramic view from the Cougals in the east to Brummies Lookout in the west includes superb views of Murwillumbah and Mt Warning. You can also look down on the canopy of the rainforest below the cliffs.

Temperate rainforests grow only at high altitudes in this region, where fertile soils have weathered from Blue Knob basalts, on the upper layers of lava on the Mt Warning shield. High rainfall of above 15 centimetres per annum is received at this altitude and these areas are frequently located in cloud. This type of forest is dominated by smaller southern species of trees which usually have very small leaves. Many large lilies grow on the forest floor and their attractive pink flowers can be seen in December. The misty conditions caused by frequent clouds promote the growth of mosses on the trunks of trees adding to the unique appearance of this plant community. This walk is worth taking even when clouds swirl through the forest obscuring the view from the lookout because of the special eerie atmosphere that these conditions lend to this rainforest.

Warrie National Park

Several interesting views and walks are available in Warrie National Park located along and below the northeastern escarpment of Springbrook Plateau. These walks tend to duplicate the experiences described for Purlingbrook Falls in Gwongorella National Park and therefore are not treated in detail in this book.

Goomoolahara Falls are located at the end of the road near the English Gardens and can be reached by a walk of approximately 150 metres. The walk to the lookout above these falls takes you through sclerophyll forest with some large wattles and a heath-like understorey similar in appearance to the forest above Purlingbrook Falls. Walk to the right (less than 100 metres) to Boojerahala Lookout for a splendid view of both the Goomoolahara Falls and down valley to the tall buildings of Surfers Paradise with the ocean beyond. Note that rainforest with its bright green canopy grows on the lower slopes and the valley floor but sclerophyll forest with a lighter green and less dense canopy occupies the upper slopes and ridge tops. Bright red flame trees can be seen in full bloom in December. The plant community surrounding Boojerahala Lookout appears to have been disturbed less frequently in the past than in the area next to the falls as it has several large New England blackbutt trees and a well-established understorey of smaller rainforest trees dominated by coachwoods.

Canyon Lookout gives perhaps the most commanding

view down over Warrie National Park, an ideal place to take people who don't wish to, or who are unable to walk, as you can drive right to and park at the lookout. This lookout is a good place to commence walking on the Twin Falls Circuit, 4 kilometres long, or the longer 17-kilometres Warrie Circuit. Further information about these walks or other walks on the Springbrook Plateau can be obtained from the Ranger's Station.

6
Lamington National Park walks

The Lamington National Park is one of the older National Parks having been gazetted in 1915, just thirty-six years after the first Australian park, the Royal National Park in Sydney. Lamington includes the highest remaining remnants of the old volcanic shield, which now form high plateaux fanning out between the streams of the old radial drainage system. The Tweed volcano was active for several million years and during that time went through several distinct phases. The most obvious change in activity was the alternation between basaltic and rhyolitic lava extrusions. The nature of these two types of lava produces distinct ecogeologic units and this group of walks is designed to allow you to investigate the close relationship between geology and ecology.

BINNA BURRA WALKS

Binna Burra Lodge is the most accessible of the walking areas in the Lamington Plateau. Its origins are closely intertwined with the origin of the National Parks movement in Australia. Two of the major figures in the genesis of Australian National Parks were the Queensland sawmiller Romeo Lahey and his assistant Arthur Groom. Arthur Groom was a major figure in the establishment of the Binna Burra Lodge and his book detailing the early days of the movement and the lodge makes very entertaining reading. The book is available at the Binna Burra Lodge store along with excellent track maps and other books and souvenirs. The Lodge is an excellent base for many of the bush walks in this section of the book. The accommodation is good, the meals well renowned, and the service excellent. However the cost may be out of your reach and you may find that camping in the well-appointed camping area/caravan park, is a better proposition. The excellent amenities include hot showers, electric barbeques and well-maintained camp sites with a lovely view.

Mt Hobwee

Binna Burra Lodge provides the starting-point for a series of well-graded walking tracks in the eastern section of Lamington National Park. The tracks lead out to the rim where there are magnificent views of almost the whole of the erosion caldera of the old Tweed volcano. The energetic can tour right through to O'Reillys along the rim, taking in a series of magical lookouts, some of which are described later in the O'Reillys' section. Mt Hobwee does not have exceptional views but is of interest because it is higher than Mt Warning. Various maps give its height at different figures but the accepted view is that it is approximately 6 metres higher than the mountain that spawned it which is 1160 metres high. The height of these ranges is hard to appreciate from the Tweed Valley as a trick of perspective makes the closer Mt Warning appear to dwarf them. This led to early confusion in the colony of Queensland. In 1828 Logan and other explorers set out to find the Tweed from the Brisbane side but kept being confused by Mt Lindesay far to the west. They did not realise that the mountains forming the backdrop to Mt Warning were almost all as high as the imposing central core, so obvious to passing ships. As a result they could not see Mt Warning from the northern side and being edged westward by the impenetrable jungles of Lamington came to view the not dissimilar outline of Mt Lindesay which they ascended on 3 August 1828. Thus they were considerably confused as that mountain was obviously not where good navigation said Mt Warning should be. Poor Captain Logan never gained much success. Hated by the convicts, derided in legend and song as a cruel monster, he was eventually speared to death by the local Aborigines.

Binna Burra White Caves

Before you leave, obtain one of the excellent self-guiding walk brochures and a track map from the kiosk. It will add greatly to your understanding and enjoyment of the walk.

Basaltic lava phases were relatively quiet with steady extrusions of fluid lava, which spread over fairly large distances. Since the average slope of the shield seems to have been only about 3° the spread of the lava must have been slow but spectacular. It seems likely that the basalts were extruded from several subsidiary vents as well as the main vent at Mt Warning.

The rhyolitic phases were much more explosive and spectacular. Acidic lavas such as rhyolite are much more viscous, they do not flow very rapidly and tend to cool and solidify close to their source. It is thought that they may tend to begin to solidify within the vent, blocking the vent until sufficient pressure has been generated to clear the blockage. This happens with explosive force causing ash and angular blocks, called 'volcanic bombs' to be ejected from the vent. This ash and debris consolidates into a rock called 'agglomerate', a term that refers to the random nature of its composition.

The trachyte mass of Egg Rock represents a subsidiary vent to Mt Warning and was the source of the rhyolite lavas in the Binna Burra area as well as the agglomerates of Bushrangers Caves and the Natural Bridge. The White Caves at Binna Burra are an especially interesting phenomenon. The are composed of tuff, that is consolidated volcanic ash, but the ash is very fine and pure. This is most unusual in tuffs, which are usually extruded in the presence of debris, and further the ash making up the tuff appears to have been water sorted. It seems that the eruption at Egg Rock dammed off a small valley on the flanks of the main volcanic shield. In the course of the eruption ash was extruded and washed into the lake, where it was laid down as a fairly thick layer. Later lava flows covered the ash and compressed and heated it until it consolidated into the rock we see in the walls of the various caves. Pitchstones and agglomerates were also part of the extrusion and can be seen in the floor and roof of the caves.

Tuff, despite its name, is not 'tough' and the tuffs near Binna Burra have been eroded into spectacular swirling caves. The available literature suggests that these caves were produced by swirling winds, however, the similarities between the shape of the caves and the shape of the water-worn swirl in the rocks at the top of the Natural Bridge suggests that the origin may have been during the erosion of the Coomera Valley. Whatever the origin of the caves you are unlikely to see anything similar elsewhere in the world.

The White Caves walk takes you across the basalt rhyolite boundary. You can easily see the differences in the vegetation of the two rock types. The rhyolite is relatively infertile and does not have the capacity of basalt to retain water. As a result the rhyolite tends to support sclerophyll forests whose trees have hard waxy leaves and other defences against dehydration that are absent in the rainforest species found on basalt in the same area.

While you are on this walk look out for the most majestic red cedar to be easily seen in the whole area reaching a height of 46 metres. It is well signposted and soars upward with breathtaking grace and symmetry. The walk is worthwhile just for the chance to view this magnificient specimen, and you gain some appreciation of why various writers speak of the 'romance of the red cedar'. Perhaps they were not referring entirely to the adventure of cedar-getting.

If you take the usual course and do the caves walk in an anti-clockwise direction you will come out near the start of another interesting trail. This is the Senses Trail, a walk set up specifically for the blind or partially sighted. A unique and rewarding experience is to do this walk on a dark night without the aid of a flashlight using only the guide rope provided. As well as gaining an insight into the world of the blind, you are also given an excellent introduction to the sensuous world of the rainforest at night.

Binna Burra——Picnic Rock

While preparing for some of the longer walks you may like to take another of the shorter walks down to Picnic Rock. This involves a stroll of 2.5 kilometres down to the edge of the rhyolite lava flows originating from Egg Rock. The rock itself is an extension of the flow that seems to hang out over the gorge cut by Nixons Creek. The views across to the Shipstern Range and down the valley to Egg Rock, the Numinbah Valley and the Gold Coast are spectacular. Of particular interest is Egg Rock, the subsidiary vent from which the rhyolite flows which give the area its character originated. The Rock bears a surprising resemblance to the Doon Doon Doughboy, the vent thought to have given rise to the rhyolite flows on the southern side of the Tweed. If you are energetic you can continue on to the foot of Ballunjui Falls and further on to the Shipstern Circuit but these double and treble the distances.

Binna Burra—Daves Creek

The Daves Creek walk at Binna Burra takes you across one of the largest areas of exposed rhyolite in the area of the old shield. The walk covers a total distance of 12.8 kilometres, but the tracks are well graded and the walking is easy. From the kiosk at Binna Burra obtain one of the track maps. There are enough tracks in the area for a walker to become confused, which could result in walking extra kilometres.

On your way out look for a small grove of Antarctic beech trees which occur on the top side of the track not long after the turnoff from the main border track. Their strange twisted and gnarled trunks are quite out of character with the rest of the rainforest.

Twig fall from the Antarctic beech is quite heavy and if you are ever caught out in cold wet weather in the Lamington, the Antarctic beech can be your salvation. Many of the small twigs get caught up in the forks of the trunks where they are kept relatively dry, making an ideal basis for that emergency fire. About 4 kilometres out the rocks change from basalt to rhyolite with a dramatic change in vegetation. The rainforest alters, seemingly, within a few steps to wet sclerophyll with New England blackbutts , tallow woods and other eucalypts. The trees are truly magnificent, consisting of some of the largest and most impressive in the area. After the diversity of the rainforest this newer simplified forest is unexpected. If you take the right-hand turn you soon find yourself in a most amazing environment. The forest quickly gives way to a type of heath and you could expect to walk out onto a beach over the next dune. In spring the area has many wildflowers in bloom.

The heath is the largest although not the only example of this response to the impoverished rhyolite bedrock. Most rhyolites support wet sclerophyll forest but here the area has been exposed to recurrent fires sweeping up through the Daves Creek Gorge. The ferocity of the fires has tipped the balance in the favour of grasses and shrubs which can recover quickly. The recurrence of the fires and the paucity of the soils prevented the establishment of the larger species. Other examples of this type of ecological system can be found on the Doon Doon Saddle and in microcosm on the top of Mt Wagawn and the Tweed Pinnacle.

From the heath there are uninterrupted views. The track winds along the edge of the Daves Creek Gorge where there are excellent views of the Numinbah Valley and across to the cliffs of Springbrook. The soils beneath your feet give a clue to the effect of the rhyolite, they are a grey colour, sandy-looking and have a very distinct clay layer which traps water and prevents it from soaking in to any great depth. As a result the surface is waterlogged in all but the driest of conditions. Along the edges of the gorge the weathering pattern common in rhyolite is easily seen particularly in the vicinity of Molongolee Cave which is very similar in formation to those on the White Caves circuit. Glimpses can even be seen of Cape Byron away to the right through the Numinbah Gap. Drinking water can usually be found on the track and there is an excellent lunch spot at the end of Surprise Rock, a residual outcrop of alkaline rhyolite.

For the energetic a walk across to the top of Ballunjui Falls covers an additional 6.5 kilometres, making the round trip 19.3 kilometres. This provides a contrast in the effects of the rhyolite. At Ballunjui Falls the rhyolite performs its normal function in creating the steep cliffs that make the waterfalls of the Lamington so spectacular and well known. Be careful when reading your map to note that the Upper Ballunjui track does not link up with the Lower Ballunjui Falls track. To make the connection between the two tracks requires a very long detour right around the Shipstern Range.

There are many other interesting walks in the Binna Burra area and the excellent camping facilities may encourage you to stay on and take in the delights of the area. Lodge staff, National Parks officers and the Lamington Natural History Association are excellent sources of information and inspiration. The new Natural History Association premises are located at the lower end of the Caves track next to the National Parks and Wildlife Service barracks. If you need more than this, the Lodge shop carries a comprehensive range of books and booklets on the natural history of the area.

O'REILLYS WALKS

The O'Reilly family came from Leura in the Blue Mountains district in 1911 and took up farmland on the edge of the Lamington Plateau. They eked out a precarious existence based on dairy farming until 1915 when, at the instigation of Romeo Lahey, a national park was proclaimed in the Lamington. The National Park boundaries virtually surrounded their property and with a strangely conservationist outlook (for farmers at that time) they rapidly switched their major activity in 1926 to a guest house for visitors to the park.

The indigenous wildlife was encouraged and protected by the family who took an intelligent, caring interest in their surroundings. One of the features of O'Reillys to this day is the lack of fear of the pademelons, crimson rosellas, satin bower birds, regent bower birds and many other wild creatures that regularly come into the Guest House area. If you have a picnic lunch there you may well find yourself disputing the rights to your sandwiches with a cheeky crimson rosella strutting across the table.

The reputation of the Guest House was well established by the time of the Stinson crash, but one of the younger sons, Bernard, wrote O'Reillys Guest House firmly into the history books as a result of the crash. On 19 February 1937 a Stinson airliner left Brisbane on its way south via Lismore and Armidale to Sydney. The weather was a bit murky and the Stinson never arrived. Reports of its whereabouts were confusing and it was officially believed that the plane had gone down in the sea off Broken Bay. Many men searched the Lamington but it fell to young Bernard to find the wreck perched on a steep slope at the head of Christmas Creek. Two men had survived and Bernard, though exhausted himself, went on to organise the rescue.

An instant national hero, Bernard was feted throughout the country as the typical Australian bushman until the war intervened and swept away the memory of his adventure. Although some in this area still remember, Bernard and the feats of his friends and neighbours have faded from the forefront of Australian history although a television documentary was produced in 1988 in memory of the aeroplane crash and the rescue. Future generations will undoubtedly rediscover this sensitive and courageous man and give him the recognition he so richly deserves. The crash was very significant, not only in the circumstances of the rescue, but also in its impact on Australian aviation. As a result of the crash new regulations were introduced into aviation forcing airline operators to install a new gadget in their aeroplanes, the radio.

O'Reillys is not easy to reach, some of the isolation still remains in the long winding road from Canungra. However the hospitality of the family and the beauty of the wildlife make the place entrancing. O'Reillys is a good place to look at the edge of the volcano. There are many walks that take you down through beautiful waterfalls created by the various lava flows and the Guest House perches on the edge of the west-facing escarpment of the plateau, with panoramic views of Brisbane's scenic rim.

Border walks

Walks of various grades and distances can be made from the Guest House. Stay a while and look around, you will find the Guest House staff and the National Parks Rangers happy to help with information and advice. Our special interest forces us to look at only the walks out to the main border lookouts.

Mt Wanungra

Wanungra Lookout is on the border track about 8 kilometres out from the Guest House. Just before you reach this peak you pass through a magnificent stand of Antarctic beeches. One of these trees is the most picturesque in the forest. Its ancient root line stands almost 3 metres above the forest floor. The attraction of this lookout is the panoramic views across the eastern part of the erosion caldera. The lookout is so close to the edge that it takes your breath away. At one time the area was frequented by a tiger cat that was so accustomed to people that it would rummage through your pack, and threaten you if you attempted to interrupt its raid.

Mt Bithongabel

West of Wanungra along the border track about 1.6 kilometres is one of the main peaks, Mt Bithongabel. The views from Bithongabel Lookout take in the deep gash of the Limpinwood Valley and sweep right across to Mt Warning with its surrounding ring dykes. From the right of the lookout as you face the valley a track drops off into the Limpinwood Valley. The track is very steep and little used and this walk is not recommended unless you are very fit and have an experienced guide. The McLennan boys from Limpinwood used this track for a night out at O'Reillys back in the days when entertainment was something that didn't come out of a power point in the wall.

The significance of Bithongabel in the Stinson saga is that Bernard rode his horse along an old bridle track to this point then proceeded on foot into the trackless jungle in the general direction of the ridges he thought the most likely site of any crash. Bernard's equipment was primitive by today's standards consisting of a loaf of bread, some tea and sugar, some onions, and a map. Onions were often the preferred food of bushmen in those days as they rot from the outside in and will even last a considerable time in the harshest conditions. A jam tin and a box of matches would have completed his kit, all safely stowed in a sugar bag.

A 6.4-kilometre walk delivers you back to O'Reillys along the track that Bernard must have taken on his way out. If you are feeling energetic and have plenty of time you can return via Echo Point, but it is a long way round if you have been to Wanungra first.

Echo Point

About 1 kilometre from Bithongabel on the direct track to O'Reillys is a turn off that takes you to a most scenic view of the middle part of the caldera. All the way down the ridge to Echo Point the track seems to skirt the edge of the sheer drop into Limpinwood, and the lookout at Echo Point seems to hang in space over this deep gash in the caldera rim.

At the point the views are fabulous, but the Limpinwood Nature Reserve cuts off views to the west and southwest. Across a deep cleft Mt Worendo and Mt Wupawn can be clearly seen, so close that you can bounce echoes off them on a still day. Evidently the Aboriginal people of the Tweed would climb the steep ridge over Mt Worendo and drop down the right branch of the Albert River to visit their friends in the Beaudesert area. One of their number, Duranbah, died on the trip down to see his mother at Fingal Heads on the coast and was buried on the lower edge of the Limpinwood Nature Reserve. His grave can be seen to this day, but various visitors have removed the bright stones that used to adorn the site.

Echo Point is an excellent place for a picnic with water close by in another branch of the Albert River. The return to O'Reillys can be made along the Lightning Falls track, a round trip of about 20 kilometres. About 100 metres along this track is a turn off that takes you away from the graded track system and into the wilderness area of the Lamington. This area is for the well equipped and experienced only, as the tracks are blazed trails and their clarity often depends on how many people have been using them recently.

There are many interesting walks originating from O'Reillys, most of which take you to beautiful waterfalls.

Track maps are available at the kiosk, and other information is available from the ranger. The camping area is well appointed but you may have difficulty getting a camp site at the most popular times, school holidays and long weekends, particularly Easter.

7
Stinson walks

The wreck of the old Stinson airliner lies on the steep slopes about 1 kilometre below Point Lookout on the slopes of the Queensland side of the ranges. This places it in about the middle of the wilderness area of the Lamington National Park. Going there is an adventure, and definitely not a relaxed stroll for a Sunday afternoon. There are several ways that you can get there and each involves considerable effort and some degree of risk. However to experience the primitive brooding forests and marvel at their pristine beauty there is no better trip.

O'Reillys——Stinson

To get to the Stinson from O'Reillys you must follow the trail of Bernard on his search. In his book Bernard says that he went to Bithongabel and then followed an old track to 'the point of echoes', obviously Echo Point. He then struck out across the grain of the land towards the west. Bernard was a bushman and knew the area very well so it is unlikely that he followed a direct course. It is more likely that he followed the rough line of the border track followed by Roberts in his original survey of the New South Wales–Queensland border. Skirting along the rim, where undulations are less steep and the going made easier by the lack of deep gorges, this route is the logical way to move across the grain of the country.

From O'Reillys take the main Border Track towards Bithongabel, and the turn off to Cominan and Echo Point. Stop at Echo Point to take in the glorious views and check your map before leaving the security of the graded track system for the uncertainty of the blazed trails in the wilderness area. About 100 metres from Echo Point there is a fairly well-marked track leading off to the left. This is often used and there is usually no difficulty in

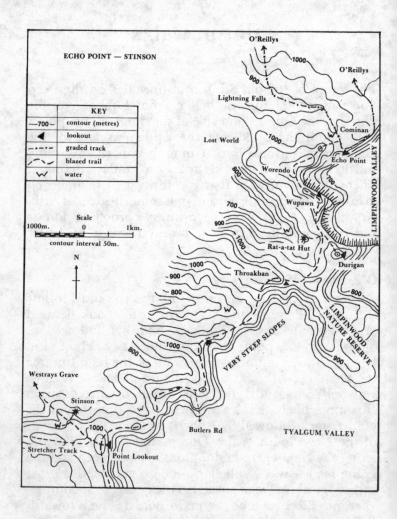

Fig. 15 The Border Track from Echo Point to the Stinson (Source 1:50,000 Tyalgum map sheet)

locating it and following it over Mt Worendo and Mt Wupawn to Rat-a-tat hut at the back of Mt Durigan. Rat-a-tat is quite a nice camping ground but being so close to the edge of the wilderness area it tends to be overused. The hut is of galvanised iron and bush pole construction and lies in a picturesque but rather damp tributary of the Albert River. Collect drinking water here as you will probably not have the chance for an hour or more. Rat-a-tat is not on the main track but it is worth taking a trip down to see since it only involves a short walk.

From Rat-a-tat you contour across the back of Mt Durigan before climbing the steep faces of the most majestic of mountains, Throakban, which Bernard O'Reilly felt should have been called the 'Cloud Maker'. Just before the summit there is a lookout which gives an excellent view of the ranges as they veer in to the west. Throakban lies at the top of the Limpinwood Nature Reserve, the range that divides the Limpinwood and Tyalgum valleys. At 1140 metres Throakban is as high as you will go on this walk and it is about as far from human habitation as you can get in the Lamington area. The top of Throakban is quite level and makes an idyllic camping spot surrounded by the ancient and mysterious Antarctic beech trees. Bernard O'Reilly slept under one of these trees and climbed another tree on this peak from where he saw a tree on a far ridge which was brown out of season. He headed for that scorched tree and found the wreck.

This area was surveyed by a most remarkable man, Queensland Government Surveyor F.E.Roberts during 1864 and 1865. As part of the border survey it was necessary to ascertain which were the divides separating the northward-flowing streams from the west and southward-flowing streams. Roberts and his men hacked their way through this country carrying chains and the other cumbersome survey equipment of the time. The whole effort was a remarkable piece of bushcraft and endurance, taking as it did the best part of two years continuously in the wilderness.

As you descend Mt Throakban look out for a short

track leading off to the right about 15 metres to a tree that still bears the markings of Roberts and his team. They measured their distances carefully with chains and marked a tree at every tenth station. Although partly overgrown by bark the letters carved into the tree by Roberts can still be faintly deciphered. They are CCCXXX but age and the healing processes of growth have all but obliterated them.

The slope down this side of Throakban seems endless but only occupies about 1 kilometre. At the bottom of the saddle water can be obtained by dropping down into a small creek and following it down, for up to a kilometre in dry weather. Navigating along this section of the border track is relatively easy as it follows the edge of the rim, however it is not so regularly walked and the track is usually quite indistinct. All along the blazed trails of the Lamington you can lose the track quite easily as there are many sharp turns for no apparent reason. In the past trees have fallen down across the track and walkers have detoured around them. The detours last much longer than the fallen tree and later walkers often blunder straight ahead, often going up to 100 metres before discovering that they are off the track. If this should happen to you don't waste your time casting around for the trail, but backtrack until you are definitely on the track then find your mistake. You will usually find that the track turned sharply around a tree and you followed the mistaken track of all those who passed before.

About 1 kilometre further down the track you will come to a pleasant lookout overlooking Middle Arm Creek. Another kilometre or so will bring you to another lookout beneath Antarctic beech trees at the top of the Butlers Road track up from Tyalgum. The views from here are not so good unless you climb down to the edge of the scarp to avoid the trees, but it is an ideal lunch spot or camp site. There is no water so make sure you pick up what you need at the foot of Throakban.

When the word about the Stinson was received in the valley, many people came up the Butlers track to view the wreck. Even the more adventurous young ladies in their long skirts or riding habits made the climb. One hundred metres below this lookout the Butlers Road track emerges over the scarp on your left. Two hours walking down the middle of the ridge and two small scrambles down rock faces would see you on the floor of the Tweed Valley. (For more details see the description in the Butlers Road Stinson Walk.) This ridge must be very close to the one from which Bernard claims to have heard 'cooees' from the direction of the 'burn't tree' he had observed from Throakban. The film 'The Riddle of the Stinson' implied that these may well have come from the imitative calls of lyrebirds. It is difficult to believe that Bernard could have heard the calls of weakened survivors at this distance. Rainforest dampens sound so well a few metres will cut out the sound of normal conversation.

The next two hours walking takes you across some lower ridges before a final steep haul up to the top of Point Lookout. When you reach the top you will find a relatively overused camp spot with a four-way track intersection. The left-hand track takes you down a 50-metre path to a precipitous lookout from which you can look down on the Tweed Valley, across to Mt Warning and to the left you can see the ridge you have traversed. This view is one of the photographs in Bernard O'Reilly's book *Green Mountains*.

Immediately down the ridge to your left is the saddle that the Stinson captain, Rex Boyden, appears to have been making for, when a downdraft caught the aeroplane and flung it down, without warning, into the trees. The plane had left Brisbane's Archerfield Aerodrome under overcast conditions, produced by a tropical low pressure system off Coffs Harbour. The aeroplane was to stop at Lismore and Armidale. In those days the planes had no 'blind' flying instruments and going up into the clouds with the mass of Mt Warning dangerously near, was fraught with danger.

Boyden, it appears, made the sensible decision to stay in visual contact with the ground and aimed for a narrow gap between cloud and ridge line. Modern theory tells us that the convergence necessary for a certain quantity of air to fit through a small opening is matched by divergence as it emerges from the gap. Additionally the air speeds up in much the same way as water through a pinched hose pipe, so Boyden's aircraft was suddenly subjected to an unexpectedly rapid blast of downdraft. His passengers reported that the pilot and co-pilot were talking and smiling in the cockpit, with the trees close below at one moment, and they hit the trees without warning the next.

The right-hand track takes you down to the emergency camp site established at the time of the crash to treat the survivors. The crash site was too steep and some time would pass before 100 brush hook-wielding bushmen could cut the stretcher track and provide a route to safety. Not far down (about 100m.) from Point Lookout you will see the old stretcher track cut off to the left. Be careful on this section of the track, it is regularly walked but follows a small creek bed for a short distance before it cuts up through a grove of Antarctic beeches and you can easily miss the point where it breaks out of the creek.

This grove of Antarctic beeches is a particularly fine example, they are so obviously ancient, and so gnarled and misshapen. The fairytale effect is heightened by the peculiar quality of the light in the afternoon when the western sun's reddish rays are reflected by the dead beech leaves on the ground giving the whole area a strange sepia tint. At other times the mist and clouds swirling in the tree tops gives a hint of surrealism and even, at times, of menace. Perhaps these feelings come from early childhood picture-books of Hansel and Gretel or Red Riding Hood or perhaps they are vestiges of some archetypal memory of the menace of forests, a hangover from our European ancestry. Perhaps they are grounded in some other phenomenon because the Aboriginal people also avoided the depths of the forests. In this case though, the avoidance can be explained in the simple fact that the rainforests provided little in the way of the day-to-day needs of life, they are wet, leech-ridden and generally nasty and unpleasant environments to live in for any length of time.

The emergency treatment site is a large barren space between the trees where the forest has not recovered from the initial clearing and the continual use by visitors to the wreck. Again three tracks lead off, water to the left, Christmas Creek ahead, and the wreck to the right. The watering point is in a particularly pretty section of a branch of Christmas Creek and well worth the effort even if you do not need to partake of its pure and refreshing water. The track to Christmas Creek goes straight down the ridge with a detour to Westray's Grave. This track is the most usual access to the wreck and is described in another section.

The right-hand track takes you from the emergency treatment site across to the wreck. When we first visited the wreck, the track was in a very degraded condition as it descended straight down to the wreck in its last 100 metres or so and was subject to rapid soil erosion. A working party established a new track for the fortieth anniversary in 1977 and also built a proper headstone for the graves of those killed in the crash. The walk across is only a few hundred metres but gives a good impression of the precipitous nature of the crash site.

All that remains of the Stinson is a mass of tangled wreckage that is the pipe frame and stub axles of the fabric-covered craft. When it went down the plane was carrying a full load of fuel, enough to get it comfortably to Sydney, and the flammability of its construction makes the survival of Westray, Binsted and Proud, little short of miraculous. The motors and other items salvaged were later carried out by pack-horse and thousands of visitors have since taken home small souvenirs of the crash.

The crash site is steeply sloping and it is easy to understand why Binsted should become exhausted after a few days of fetching water from the creek below. He was fortunate to find a container in the wreck, the outside of a thermos now preserved in Beaudesert's museum. This piece of good luck probably saved Proud's life. Without it they would have had to move away from the wreck making their discovery much less likely. The distance to the nearest settlement is only a few kilometres and the survivors expected help to arrive within a few hours. James Westray had experience walking and mountaineering in Wales and after one night had passed he decided to go for help. The other two, being convinced that help would come, decided to remain where they were. Unfortunately for them the captain of a coastal vessel had reported that they flew overhead just north of Sydney and the main search was being concentrated in that area. Westray died on the way out almost within sight of help and the other two huddled on the mountainside for ten days giving a 'cooee' every half-hour or so to guide any rescuers. When Bernard found them their first concern appears to have been the fate of Don Bradman in his innings at Melbourne Cricket Ground. Perhaps they needed most of all to be reminded that the world was still normal after what was an extremely harrowing experience.

Imagine the scene, Proud badly injured and in considerable pain, the other two badly shocked and carrying their own injuries. The hope turning to despair, firstly of an early rescue and secondly of a successful outcome of Westray's foray in search of aid. If you have sat in the rainforest waiting for someone for any length of time you will remember how the ordinary sounds of the forest take on new meanings. That bird's call is the 'cooee' of a rescue party, not far away but, unable to find you, the crackling of bushes perhaps heralds the arrival of help? Binsted certainly saved Proud's life by staying with him. Whether he would have saved Westray's life by accompanying him is a matter of useless conjecture.

The simple monument erected in 1977 records the details of the disaster with brass plaques for those who died. When we first went there in 1975 there was only a wooden cross commemorating the burial place of the remains of the captain. After forty years his memory was still kept by his relatives. The power of the place is its atmosphere, not the atmosphere of death or angry ghosts but the atmosphere of ghosts filled with the joy of living. The ghostly images of courage, responsibility, and enduring mateship seem to bridge the years.

This trip will take you at least two days so you will need to camp out for the night. The site of the emergency treatment station is unpleasant, it is damp, depressing, and very much overused. It would be far preferable to camp back at Point Lookout where you have the view of the sunrise to look forward to and the comfort of sleeping on level ground. For your return trip you can retrace your steps or perhaps more sensibly take one of the other available routes, provided that you can arrange your transport suitably.

Wiangarie——Stinson

An alternative route to the Stinson wreck is from the Tweed Valley Lookout. This lookout is on the Tweed Range Scenic Drive in the Border Ranges National Park, formerly Wiangarie State Forest. Take the Gradys Creek track from the edge of the road, about 1 kilometre west of the Tweed Valley Lookout. The start of the track used to be well signposted and once carried a sign labelled 'Stinson'. The uncertain nature of the track and some people getting lost in the area led the NSW National Parks to remove the sign to discourage walkers, now all that remains is a tunnel-like opening into the weeds on the edge of the forest. Do not attempt this walk unless

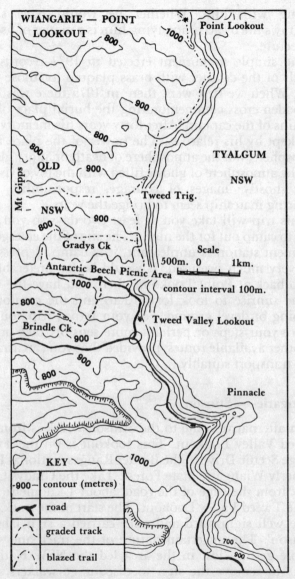

WIANGARIE — POINT LOOKOUT

Point Lookout

QLD
NSW

TYALGUM

NSW

Mt Gipps

Tweed Trig.

Gradys Ck

Antarctic Beech Picnic Area

Scale

500m.   0   1km.

contour interval 100m.

Brindle Ck

Tweed Valley Lookout

Pinnacle

KEY

-900-	contour (metres)
∿	road
- - -	graded track
-·-·-	blazed trail

Fig. 16 Track map of the Border Track from the Tweed Range to Point Lookout (Source 1:50,000 Tyalgum sheet)

you are familiar with the blazed trails of the Lamington Wilderness area, as you can easily lose the track and be the embarrassed subject of a search.

Follow the track across to Gradys Creek and then take the turn-off to the Border Track. The junction of these tracks is marked with a sign pointing to the Richmond Gap one way and the Stinson the other. Take the main Border Track from here eastwards to Point Lookout, about three to five hours away. This track is often very indistinct and has many unexpected twists and turns. Follow the blaze marks, being sure to return to the point at which you were sure you were on the track if you should lose your way. Once having established your location on the track you can then look for your error in the sure knowledge that your way back is secure. You will normally find that the track has taken an unexpected turn behind a tree and escaped your notice.

On the last ridge before you come to the steady uphill climb to Point Lookout the track passes through a cleft rock. Not long after this (about 1 kilometre) you may come to a sign on a tree pointing to a divergent track to Tyalgum Valley Lookout. At the time of writing many of the signs had been removed so do not rely on finding a sign here, the track goes off to the left up to the top of Tyalgum Bluff. The lookout is worth visiting if you find the track. When the authors first visited the spot it was clear of vegetation and provided a superb view of the upper valleys of the Rous River across to Mt Warning. The last time it was visited weeds had infested the area and it was difficult to get to a position where the best views could be obtained.

Not far along the track is the junction with a track leading up from Stoddarts Road on the valley floor. Again this track used to be marked with a sign but do not rely on it being there now. This leads straight down the cliffs and is very indistinct and has several wire climbs where Jack Willows has put up fencing wire to aid walkers climbing up some quite steep sections. The

Stoddarts Road walk is described elsewhere in the text but is not recommended for the inexperienced or unaccompanied. We once spent several hours casting about along a cliff line for a way down while all the time being within sight of our waiting transport and the patient drivers. In this instance the problem was solved by slinging a rope down the cliff and climbing down to a track marker that could be seen but not reached by any other means. Interestingly the confusion was created by following blazes. The blazes had been cut by a group which was lost like us. (Fortunately the practice of cutting blazes has been replaced by the use of non-adhesive tape tied loosely to a shrub or vine at about eye level. Tape markers may be removed if you inadvertently take the wrong turn.) The blazes led to a cliff line that looked vaguely familiar and falling rocks from the cliffs above had created what looked to be blazes on the trees at the base of the cliff. We followed these for some time before becoming aware of the situation.

From this intersection the track leads steadily uphill to Point Lookout and you can proceed as outlined in the O'Reillys——Stinson walk. The advantage of this walk is that like the track from O'Reillys you begin with most of the altitude already climbed in your car. Despite this there are still some steep pinches where the track crosses the dry valleys of the old radial drainage streams. The walk can be done easily in one day, but it is about six to ten hours walking with no margin for major navigational errors. Do not try this walk if you are unfit, inexperienced, alone or frightened of the bush.

Butlers Road——the Stinson

(*Warning*. The first few hundred metres of this track crosses private property and you would be advised to gain permission before attempting this walk.)

For the adventurous and fit this walk offers the experience of climbing through the various ecological zones of the caldera walls. Go through Tyalgum past the hotel and follow the road out of the village westward until you come to the Butlers Road turn-off. Take the turn into Butlers Road and follow it to the upper reaches of the valley. You will come to a gate on your right-hand side just before a creek crossing. Leave your car here. You have to cross private property to the forest line so stop and let the residents know you are passing through.

From the gate go west to the ridge line and follow the crest to the forest line where you will find a gate in the fence. From here it is all uphill for the next four hours so establish a nice easy pace. The track is easy to follow as it negotiates the centre of a relatively narrow ridge crest. As long as you stay on the crest you are on the right track.

After a steep climb through secondary regrowth of box trees with an understorey of lantana, crofton weed and other understorey dwellers you will be blocked by a small cliff. Climb up and around to the right along a narrow ledge till you reach the crest of the ridge once more. The track flattens out here and you pass through a zone of fire-tolerant species. Grasstrees and brush box are the main large species along this dry and exposed section.

As the track begins to climb once more you will come across more and more rainforest species in the dry sclerophyll/rainforest boundary zone. Nearer the cliffs runoff and seepage from above creates a damper and more fire-resistant environment where the natural balance alternates between favouring the sclerophyll and the rainforest trees. By the time you reach the cliff line you are in easily recognisable rainforest.

At the cliff line the track will take you around to the right to a tree with a galvanised iron arrow pointing upwards. This is only about a 100 metres and is just past a tight squeeze through a cleft between fallen rocks and the cliff. Climb up the cliff, using the fencing wire if necessary, until you regain the centre of the ridge.

Be sure to have a good look around so that you will recognise that point on the way back.

The track will now take you up the centre of the ridge to the intersection with the Border Track. Turn left and you will take about two hours to reach Point Lookout, as described in the O'Reillys section. On your way back be careful near the bottom of the ridge where it divides into two, the left-hand track takes you through dense undergrowth and is to be avoided if possible. The walk will take from four to five hours each way depending on your level of fitness, but is by far the easiest route to the Stinson from the valley floor.

When the Stinson went down and word eventually reached the people of the Tweed many of the adventurous young people of the time went to view the crash site by this route. In those days the bottom slopes were much clearer and it was possible to ride almost to the first cliff line.

Stoddarts Road——the Stinson

(*Warning.* The first kilometre or so of this track crosses private property and you would be advised to gain permission before attempting this walk.)

If you proceed as for Butlers Road but continue on to the next turn you can make another climb to the top of the caldera walls. Follow the road to the end and make your way across the terraces to the point of the left-hand bluff. This section of the walk is long and tiring and best not done in the heat of the day, so get an early start. Again you are crossing private property so it would be polite to let them know you are passing through.

Cross over the small creek on the top terrace and at the point of the bluff you will find a gap through the lantana. Go through the gap and pick up the blazes on the trees. The track is very steep and as a result is not particularly popular, accordingly it is relatively indistinct and best attempted with a person who has been before. There are three sections where wire has been strung to help walkers climb steep rock sections.

The walk brings you out on the Border Track (a blazed trail only) in the saddle to the west of Point Lookout, about a half-hour's walk away. This track is much shorter but you have to climb the cliffs to reach the top. At the junction with the Border Track turn right to the Stinson and left to Tyalgum Valley Lookout as described in the Wiangarie——Stinson walk. Care will need to be taken at the top of the Stoddarts Road track as the intersection with the Border Track may be indistinct, depending on the amount of traffic it has had recently.

Westray's Grave——the Stinson

The rescue of the Stinson crash survivors was organised and co-ordinated from the Queensland side. Bernard knew the people of Christmas Creek and Lamington very well and it was natural for him to look for help in this area. If you drive through Beaudesert to Lamington village and continue through the village you will come to Stinson Park next to Lamington National Fitness Centre. Apart from the memorial there are picnic facilities with toilets and barbeques. Camping is allowed but there are no showers. The nearby creek provides a cool dip and water for a tub scrub for the hardy. From the park you can approach the Stinson from two directions. The usual route for day-walkers is via Westray's Grave, but it is also possible to follow the route of the Stretcher Track.

Westray's Grave is a very pretty spot on the banks of Christmas Creek near where James Westray died. There was much controversy at the time about where he would be buried. His family wanted the body carried out and buried in consecrated ground, but the local policeman on whom the duty would fall was less than enthusiastic. Westray's body had been out in the February sun for several days and was in an advanced state of decomposition. Eventually the problem was resolved by taking a clergyman in to the site and having him consecrate a place for the grave. Just finding a site for the grave was difficult enough as Westray died in a very steep and rocky section of the Christmas Creek gorge.

The grave site is on a small terrace covered with a bangalow palm glade. With the murmur of the creek as it glides through the rocks and slides over the nearby falls and rapids the site is idyllic, the sort of place we would all like to be buried. The one discordant note is in the wording of the headstone with its old English verbosity. Perhaps this is a personal whim but the headstone would seem more in keeping with the site and the fate of its owner if it were simple. The account of the finding of his body by O'Reilly suggests that he met his lonely fate with dignity, and O'Reilly certainly had no doubt about his bravery.

To get to Westray's Grave take the road that continues up the valley to the locked gate. From the gate follow the road for about 5 kilometres to the entrance to the National Park, crossing the creek four times. The track follows the creek for about a further 3 kilometres before you reach the grave site. Take your swimming costume in warm weather as there are some delightful swimming holes just below the grave site.

The track up to the Stinson goes up the ridge to the right through dry sclerophyll forest. It is steep and a long walk so make sure you have plenty of time. Do not attempt it in wet weather. We remember this track as a seemingly unending mudslide that sapped strength and created dangers through the unsteady footing. In dry times it is the easiest route to the crash site.

You emerge in the rescue clearing after four hours or more of steady uphill climbing with a couple of small cliff scrambles for variety. The track is well defined and is probably the main access for tourists wishing to visit the crash site. Walk on to Point Lookout to see the magnificent Antarctic beech trees and the beautiful views from the lookout. Your return can be made either by the track you ascended or by taking the Stretcher Track. The Stretcher Track is not often walked and is overgrown and long without the benefit of views. Although it is fairly level over most of its length, the extra distance deters most walkers. If you take the Stretcher Track you will come out on the ridge west of the Fitness Camp and drop down to the right into Gap Creek where a farm road will bring you back to Stinson Park.

You will notice that the vegetation of the Beaudesert side of the Lamington is quite different to the Tweed side. The communities in the valleys on the Beaudesert side resemble more closely those of the drier inland. This arises as so many other things do as a direct result of the influence of the remains of the old volcano. Geographers refer to this type of area as a 'rainshadow'. The moist easterly air streams which flow onto the coast and bring us rain are intercepted by the ranges and robbed of their moisture. The moisture that makes possible the rainforests of the Tweed and Lamington is stolen by the ranges, leaving the Beaudesert region fairly aptly named.

The Stinson walks as a whole are very strenuous owing to the isolation and precipitous nature of the country. They are recommended to the young and the fit or the dedicated as one of the better ways to experience the real sense of wilderness and adventure in walking the most inaccessible parts of the caldera. Their special historic connotations make them of additional interest, but the serious student can discover much about the ecological relationships of the Tweed volcano without venturing quite so far from civilisation.

Before you leave you will need to contact Queensland National Parks and obtain a permit to camp in the wilderness. You should let them know where you are going and how long you intend to be out in case a search is required. It must be emphasised that the Stinson is located in the middle of the Lamington Wilderness, definitely not an area to venture into without serious preparation and at least a little experience of the conditions. There are no official tracks and for most of the time you are at least six arduous hours away from any form of reliable aid.

8
Tweed Range walks

Wiangarie State Forest was incorporated in the Border Ranges National Park on its proclamation in 1983. The area comprises 30,712 hectares of that section of the caldera rim which continues to the west of the Lamington Plateau. Another name commonly used in reference to the area is the Tweed Range and National Parks literature refers to it as such. There are many interesting walks in this area which is geographically and ecologically contiguous with Lamington.

Excellent picnic spots are provided at The Bar Mountain, The Blackbutts, and at Brindle Creek. There are breathtaking views of the caldera from Blackbutts Lookout, The Pinnacle, the Tweed Valley Lookout and the Antarctic Beech Picnic Area (the last providing a chance to view the radiating ridges of the Lamington). Camping is provided for at Forest Tops Rest Area with a covered cooking area, tank water, firewood, and toilets all available. The Bar Mountain has been developed as a major day-tourist area for picnic parties only. There is a bush camping facility associated with a walk out to a spectacular lookout but you must carry packs about 2 kilometres from the picnic area to camp there.

Access to the Tweed Range area can be achieved by two routes which make up a loop. From the Kyogle—Woodenbong Road turn-off into Lynchs Creek Road at the village of Wiangaree (12.5km from Kyogle). A former forestry road takes you to Forest Tops and onto the Scenic Drive. From the Murwillumbah——Kyogle Road turn off at Lillian Rock (44km from Murwillumbah) towards Barkers Vale. A steep and winding former forestry road takes you up the western side of the ranges to The Bar Mountain and onto the Scenic Drive. Neither of these two drives should be attempt d in wet weather but if you are caught on top by rain the Lynchs Creek Road would be the preferable route out, as the Barkers Vale

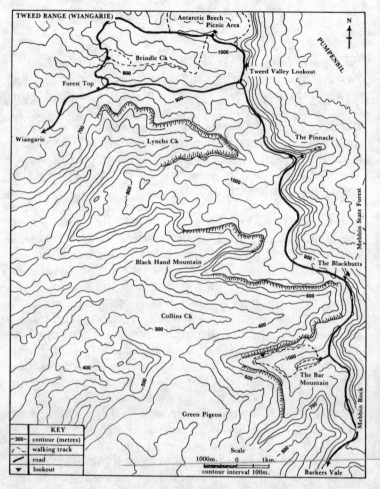

*Fig. 17 Walks in the Tweed Ranges area (Source: Tyalgum
1:50,000 sheet)*

Road is very steep with precipitous drops at the roadside.
The whole loop through Barkers Vale to Lynchs Creek
and back via Kyogle is about 102 kilometres, all but a

few of these being on dirt roads. In general the National Parks roads are kept in better condition than the shire roads, so do not be put off by the state of the early sections of the access roads.

National Parks recommends that you enter from Lillian Rock and treat the circuit as a one-way loop. Your trip takes you across poor grazing land on rocks of the older basement sedimentaries. The National Park begins at the foot of the range, and the road generally improves from this point. When the area was still being logged a sign at this point asked drivers to stop, turn their engine off and listen for the sound of timber trucks. Meeting a loaded timber truck half-way down the steep descent was frightening.

The Bar Mountain

As you climb up the ranges the atmosphere becomes cooler and the vegetation gradually changes from dry sclerophyll to wet sclerophyll types and finally into rainforest. At the top of the range a turn off to the left will take you 50 metres to The Bar Mountain picnic area. This area has two short walks that allow you to observe Antarctic beech trees without the usual climb. Two interesting aspects of the Antarctic beeches can be seen here. The first and possibly the most interesting is the beech orange. This fungus grows on the upper branches of trees in the *Menzii* pollen group of beeches found in Argentina, Chile, New Zealand, and Australia. The spores of this fungus are spread by raindrops, only a few feet at a time and it is difficult to account for their wide distribution unless you take into account continental drift which would allow these areas to have been physically joined at some point in the past.

Another interesting aspect of the beech groves is specially provided for at Bar Mountain. The Falcorostrum Loop Walk (750m.) celebrates the orchid *Dendrobium falcorostrum* which grows almost exclusively on the Antarctic beech at the summit of the ranges. The orchid flowers in early spring with large white and purple blossoms. The beech orchid as it is commonly called is quite rare and is considered an endangered plant so look but leave them alone. The Bar Mountain had special significance for the local Aboriginal tribe, the Gullibal. Areas on the summit were used as initiation sites and prospective initiates would be expected to survive alone in the forest for some time, in a sort of pilgrimage or retreat into isolation as is common in so many religious systems. The Bar Mountain is about 1100 metres above sea level and is often shrouded in cloud and mist. The rainfall is reported to be 3 to 3.5 metres per annum and snow has been reported so take your jumpers even in summer. The walks are short and suitable for all ages and all levels of fitness. Picnic tables, barbeques, and toilets are provided.

A newer, longer walk has been constructed out along the edges of the rhyolite to a spectacular lookout over Collins Creek. Take the northern track past the toilets down an old snig track which swings back to the west as it encounters the cliffs in the rhyolite. The track is well made and graded so that apart from its length it presents few difficulties. Most of the outward trip is downhill as it wends its way along the steep upper cliff area. Eventually you will come to a well-constructed lookout giving fine views out over Collins Creek to the ridge called Blackhand Mountain which is the northern much larger version of The Pinnacle. Before you get to the lookout you will pass an area set aside for bush camping. There are no facilities here but there is fresh running water from springs. After leaving the lookout the track begins to wind upwards through areas which were heavily logged in the not so distant past. The contrast between the natural areas and the logged areas is seen in the lack of large trees and the weed-clogged former snigging tracks and logging roads. Eventually the track rejoins the Falcorostrum Loop Walk bringing you back to the picnic area. The walk is about 5 kilometres in distance and should take about three hours.

Blackbutts Picnic Area

About 3.5 kilometres further along the Scenic Drive you can stop your car and look across a deep ravine to where Collins Creek plunges 150 metres to the valley floor. Less than 1 kilometre further along the road you will come to the most accessible lookout across the caldera. At The Blackbutts you can drive your car right up to the edge of the escarpment. Directly below the lookout is Mebbin Forest and across the Upper Tyalgum Valley stands Mt Warning while away to the right rises the Nightcap Ranges separated from the Tweed Range by the Nimbin Gap. This gap is the result of the erosion of the old volcano by the upper reaches of the Richmond River but long since the Tweed has undercut it and stolen its waters leaving the gap as the only remnant of a once large stream. Picnic tables, barbeques, toilets, tank water, and firewood are all provided as well as a fenced lookout deck. The area is named after some magnificent New England blackbutts that grow around the lookout site. Take your binoculars for a better view of the canopy of the forest below and the other points of scenic interest in the valley.

The Pinnacle

The most spectacular landform of the Tweed is just 7.5 kilometres further along the road. Stop at The Pinnacle carpark for one of the most unforgettable sights on the ranges. A 200-metre walk takes you over the top of the ridge and reveals the incredible Pinnacle below you, framed by the valley. If you are adventurous and have a reasonable head for heights you can walk right down onto the tip of The Pinnacle itself. This is an unforgettable experience and is not really dangerous provided you take your time and go carefully. Allow yourself plenty of time. It can take two to three hours for a walk that appears to be only a few hundred metres. The Pinnacle has a dry heath type of vegetation owing to its exposed location. Fires have regularly swept the area in the past but in recent times the absence of fire has allowed heath and young seedlings to gain a foothold. The neck of The Pinnacle is quite narrow but safe to cross and the point is small but can accommodate a small party without risk. At times we have encountered small children with their parents and very old people who have all made the trip without undue difficulty, so take yourself out to the tip for a truly unique experience. Go slow and be careful for there are definite opportunities to do yourself real harm. The track goes straight ahead from the top lookout and is well marked from the erosion caused by the many visitors who make the pilgrimage.

Tweed Valley Lookout

The road winds down behind the ridge for about 3 kilometres before cutting back to the edge of the scarp. Your next landmark is an intersection where the road turns off to the left to Forest Tops. There is no need to take this turn as the road you are on is a loop road and will eventually bring you to Forest Tops via Brindle Creek. A little further on is the Tweed Valley Lookout, where a fine view back towards The Pinnacle unfolds with the upper valley as a backdrop. Make sure you go this far even if you do not intend to explore the area further. It will give you a good impression of where you have been.

Antarctic Beech Picnic Area

This area was formerly a helicopter pad when troops from Canungra Jungle Training camp were flown in for exercises. (These exercises ceased in 1973.) There is plenty of space as the area has been used as a quarry and picnic facilities are provided. As the name implies there are Antarctic beeches (sometimes called negrohead beeches) in the immediate vicinity of the picnic area. The view away to the north is across Gradys Creek to the McPherson Ranges which are the ridge immediately across the valley of Gradys Creek. Beyond the McPhersons are the many radiating ridges of the Lamington. The Stinson is located on the far side of the third ridge to the north. From this lookout a track leads off to the left which will take you down to the Brindle Creek Picnic Area.

Brindle Creek

The track leading down into Brindle Creek passes through some very interesting forest. The walk is not steep and should be easily accomplished in two to three hours. After initially dropping down to the creek the track follows the right-hand bank down to the road bridge and picnic area at Brindle Creek. The valley is quite deep and the track for the most part is well above the creek bed, coming down to creek level occasionally as it crosses tributaries. Each time it crosses a tributary there is a small stand of Antarctic beech trees growing at the apex of the interfluve. These are among the healthiest beeches you will see anywhere in the Lamington or Tweed Ranges areas. They are also among the lowest of the beech stands, extending as they do right down almost to the Brindle Creek. Their location and persistence in this area would seem to be a key element in any effort to understand the distribution of this most interesting plant.

About half-way down you will come across a very pretty set of falls, not spectacularly large, but very scenic. Their presence will be revealed by the gurgling sound of the water cascading over the rocks. You can easily approach either the top or the bottom of these falls with only a minor scramble over a soil embankment. The pool at the base is fairly large and if patient you may see quite large specimens of the Lamington blue crayfish and eels gliding gracefully but warily among the stones and debris on the floor of the pool. You may also come across the crayfish wandering about on the tracks where, if disturbed, they will put on a marvellous display of hissing and pincer-waving. For a good photograph back them into a corner and occupy their attention with a stick, they will remain quite still for a considerable period of time. Do not be too brave near their pincers, they are designed to do more than to threaten.

Eventually you will wind down on a well-constructed track to link up with the track system originating at the Brindle Creek Picnic Area. The best way to do this walk is to arrange to have a vehicle left at the Brindle Creek Picnic Area and another to drive you to the Tweed Valley Lookout. This obviously avoids the trek back across ground already covered and has the additional advantage of allowing you to tackle the wilder section while you are fresh, and enjoy the very civilised National Parks tracks when you are feeling tired. The walk is not difficult and can be attempted by quite young children and the not-so-fit provided that sufficient time is allowed. The Gradys Creek track is of similar length and re-emerges from the forest just beyond the Antarctic Beech Picnic Area, on the road down to Brindle Creek. Gradys Creek is of particular interest to the botanically minded as it had the status of a flora reserve before the area was gazetted as a national park.

Gradys Creek

About 2 kilometres before you reach the Antarctic Beech Picnic Area you will pass a tunnel-like track entrance. This track leads off to the right and takes you across the top of the Gradys Creek Flora Reserve to the Tweed Trig from whence you can go north to the Stinson or west to Mt Gipps and the Richmond Gap. Follow the sometimes indistinct path along the ridge towards the scarp. The state of the track will depend on the frequency of its use which in turn depends upon recent weather conditions. If it has been fine for an extended period the track will be clear, however if the weather has been wet you will need to follow blaze marks and tape track-markers left by bushwalking clubs. The track soon begins to descend into the upper reaches of Gradys Creek. There is usually drinking water available where you cross the creek. Continue over the hill and you will come to an old forestry signpost which has decayed badly. It points up the hill to the Tweed Trig and the Stinson and downhill into Gradys Creek.

The walk down Gradys Creek is very similar to the Brindle Creek walk. Once again the steep sides of the creek bed force the track up onto the lower slopes and once again the chief difficulty is crossing the tributary creeks with their colonies of Antarctic beech. Several of the creek crossings are quite indistinct and you will have to cast around to find the track on the far side of the crossing. Near the bottom of the walk you will pass through a group of beeches on the creek bank and the track will seem to disappear. When the creek is flowing well you may have to go about 25 metres to your left to find a place where you can cross without wading. The track then winds up over the ridge for about 100 metres until you reach the creek again. This time it is plunging down a cascade about 20 metres in height. These are the Caves Creek Falls named on the sign back at the head of Gradys Creek. Sit on the rocks in the sun and eat your lunch or if you wish have a dip in the circular plunge pool at the bottom right of the cascades.

The beautiful clear water, the peace, and the pleasure of the sun on your face after more than two hours in the forest make this spot delightful. When you are ready to leave cross the creek at the top of the falls and follow a fairly clear track up the ridge to the road about a half-hour's walk away. From there, a left turn and 20 minutes walk will bring you to the Antarctic Beech Picnic Area and a further twenty minutes will see you back at your starting-point. A sensible way to do this walk is to leave your car at the Antarctic Beech Picnic Area and walk to the track start. This will split the fairly unexciting road sections into smaller walks at the beginning and end of the main walk. If you do have two vehicles and know the points where the walk leaves and returns to the road you can arrange your transport to avoid walking on the road at all. However the road walks give you a chance to settle into a rhythm before the walk and to wind down at the end.

From the Antarctic Beech Picnic Area the road winds down through lush forest to Brindle Creek approximately 5 kilometres away. Brindle Creek is amongst the most beautiful rainforest areas to be seen in Australia. The initial impression the area makes is poor but stop and have a look around. From the parking area immediately across the bridge a track leads off to the left. About 50 metres down this track is a second picnic spot underneath the tall trees with the creek gurgling across a stony bed nearby.

From just before this idyllic spot a track leads up the creek a short distance then crosses the creek to come back to the picnic area in a short but amazingly beautiful walk. Along the way you pass Antarctic beeches that perch out over the creek where erosion has undercut them. The beauty and quiet serenity of the forest here matches anything you are likely to find around the caldera. The track down from the Tweed Valley Lookout joins up with this loop track near the point where you cross the creek.

When you emerge at the roadside again you will see that a track begins at the opposite side of the road. This is another track of only a few hundred metres which takes you down to one of the larger and prettier red cedars to be found in the area. The picnic area has been set up to cater for large groups with many barbeques and picnic tables, firewood, toilets, and the pure running water of the creek. The firewood is often damp so if you intend to have a barbeque take along some dry firewood to allow you to start a fire with a minimum of fuss and bother.

From Brindle Creek the road winds up the ridge to Forest Tops where it re-joins the Tweed Range Scenic Drive. Turn right to Lynchs Creek or left to return to Barkers Vale. Forest Tops is the camping area provided by the National Parks and Wildlife Service. The area is quite large and well grassed, a covered cooking area is provided as well as toilets and tank water. There are no showers so be prepared for a tub scrub. One of the chief delights of this area is the people you meet. At different times we have struck a university team doing a wildlife survey, a Californian expert on staghorns, and a snake expert, all of whom were prepared to share their expertise with anyone interested enough to ask. When the area was still part of the State Forest we preferred to camp down in Brindle Creek but the increased numbers of people now using the park make this impossible.

About twenty minutes' drive down the road is the Sheepstation Creek camping ground which is not so likely to be wet and cold. Following this road out brings you to either Kyogle or Beaudesert via the scenic Lions Road. If you take the Lions Road be sure to stop and check out the Border Loop where the railway line describes a complete circle to gain altitude and reduce the length of the tunnel under the Richmond Gap. If you are well organised you can check the train timetables and arrange to be there when a train is on the loop. The area is an important part of the history of Australia and one day someone will write of the project and the huge number of men who laboured to connect the two States by rail.

The Tweed Range is beautiful and the easy accessibility of the area makes it ideal for people who are interested in the forests of the old volcano but do not have the fitness or the expertise to venture into the more inaccessible areas. Before you go be sure to obtain some of the excellent brochures available from the National Parks and Wildlife Service of NSW. Consider carefully an overnight stay as the beauty of the area cannot be fully appreciated in one rushed day-trip. You can camp out of your car and perhaps watch the sun rise from one of the lookouts.

9
Nightcap Range walks

The Nightcap Range is the lowest and most severely eroded of the three huge plateaux forming the western-half of the caldera rim. The more elevated parts of this range, exceeding 900 metres at Mt Burrell, were never cleared for farming. This forest-clad plateau has long been the source of timber for the sawmilling industries of both the Tweed and Richmond valleys. Selective logging has removed most of the commercially valuable timber from this area but has not removed the forests from the more elevated parts. Pressure from conservation groups and a declining supply of logs available to the timber industry led to a change in government policy towards rainforests in New South Wales and the proclamation of the Nightcap National Park on the western part of the plateau including the Historic Nightcap Track, the Terania Creek basin and Mt Burrell. The eastern part of the plateau is still managed as State Forest. Both areas contain interesting bushwalks.

Mt Nardi (altitude 815 metres) is one of the highest peaks in the Nightcap National Park and is the site for two television transmitters 12 kilometres north of the small town of Nimbin. Take the Tuntable Falls road east of Nimbin and then proceed north on Newton Drive which climbs the ridge of Konorigan Range. The huge transmitting towers dominate the skyline at this point. Picnic facilities have been established in a small park between the two transmitters but, as yet, no camping facilities have been provided. A viewing platform has been constructed on the southern side of the larger ABC transmitter, giving a spectacular view of the Richmond Valley. This is possibly the largest area of land that you can view from any one lookout in the region. The panoramic view includes Lismore and the interesting Nimbin Rocks. A network of walking tracks leads off into the forest from the northern side of the smaller commercial transmitter.

Mt Nardi——Mt Matheson

A short loop track links Mt Nardi to Mt Matheson 1 kilometre away. Other tracks branch off this track and lead to Pholis Gap Lookout in the west and Tuntable Falls and the Nightcap Track in the east. Unfortunately several large trees, located near Mt Nardi, have suffered from dieback, demonstrating just how fragile natural ecosystems are when surrounded by development. This track takes you through subtropical rainforest on this warm northerly slope, in spite of the fact that the altitude exceeds 800 metres on these peaks. The track turns to the right at the junction with the track to Pholis Lookout.

The track now follows the rim to the east through a viny scrub type of rainforest at the exposed edge of the caldera. From time to time you emerge out into the blackbutt-dominated forest on the very edge of the escarpment. The track at this point takes you through the boundary zone between the two types of forest. Tantalising views elude you as you attempt to peer to the north through the scrub suggesting the reward in store for you at the next lookout. The loop track branches off to the left at one of the most magnificent flame trees you will see. This tree is a spectacular sight when in bloom.

As you descend over the rim of the caldera the forest quickly changes to sclerophyll forest and heath on bands of less fertile rhyolite. The track can be remarkably wet even in dry weather, from water seeping from a spring line at the base of the basalt layer above. Two distinctive old tree stumps bear witness to the forestry techniques of the past. The notches cut into their trunks show how the cutters climbed them to cut them down with a cross-cut saw several metres above the ground. A nearby stump cut at waist-level demonstrates how much easier the

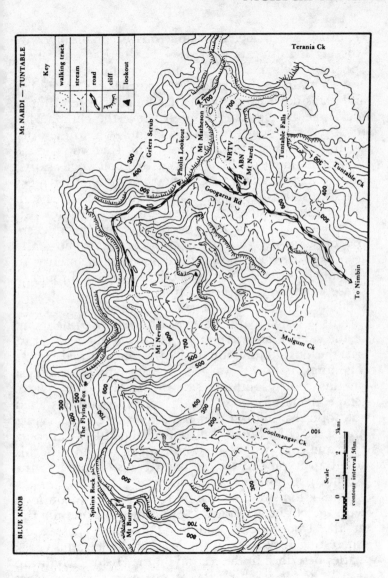

Fig. 18 Map of the Nightcap Range in the Blue Knob, Mt Nardi area

chainsaw has made this dangerous occupation today. Another log appears to lie exactly where it was felled, apparently when cut it was found to be unsuitable.

A short track (five minutes) branches off to the left and leads down to a spectacular lookout perched on a rock, like an eagle's eerie high above the cliffs . This track passes down through the rainforest into the drier sclerophyll forest on the exposed rim. Here you can see some remarkable old blackbutts with broad woody skirts, quite magnificent trees. On the rhyolite band of rocks that forms the ridge the soils are thin and a tea-tree heath and grasstree association is the dominant vegetation. An interesting aspect of the grasstrees is that near where the forest ends staghorns and crows nest ferns, normally seen high in the canopy, have attached themselves to the much lower grasstrees. You pass down through a dense stand of grasstrees to a final precipitous, but short scramble to the lookout perched on the edge of the cliffs.

This is probably the best view from the southern rim of the caldera and certainly well worth the walk. Just past the lookout junction the loop rejoins the main track. The forest is now a warm temperate type of rainforest on this cooler southerly side of Mt Matheson. Warm temperate rainforest grows in cooler conditions than subtropical rainforest and lacks the large woody vines and spectacular buttressed roots of the latter. Calicoma trees and coachwoods are dominant in this area. In this small area you can see the main types of forest in the Nightcap living in close proximity.

An 8-kilometre track connects the Mt Matheson loop with the Nightcap Track, joining this track on the rim at the Doon Doon Saddle. This track passes the interesting rock spire at the head of the Terania Creek Valley described in the section on the Historic Nightcap Track. Before reaching the rock spire a track branches to the right and leads down the ridge between Terania and Tuntable creeks. Another right-hand turn will take you across to the top of the Tuntable Falls, a large set of falls similar to the Protestors Falls and Minyon Falls further to the east. This track is not as well marked as the others nearer Mt Nardi and care will be needed.

Pholis Gap walk

Athol Pholi was killed in the area when felling a tree, one of the more dangerous occupations in Australia. Pholis Gap was named in his memory. Pholis walk is a short track, 1.5 kilometres long, linking the gap with the Mt Matheson Track, commencing at a left turn 600 metres from Mt Nardi. This is a self-guided walk designed to give information about the environment, with stopping-points marked by numbered pegs. Information pamphlets are available at Mt Nardi explaining various features to be seen at each peg. The walk descends through rainforest to sclerophyll forest as fertile red soils on the Blue Knob basalts give way to poorer soils on rhyolite at lower altitudes near the gap.

As indicated earlier the track commences in luxurious subtropical rainforest with many fine examples of buttressed roots and woody vines. At one place the track crosses an abandoned forestry road, an excellent place to observe the regeneration processes at work, as nature repairs the damage caused by clearing. Young seedlings are re-establishing the rainforest here. The track now follows this abandoned road and the associated drainage works.

The forest quickly changes to the sclerophyll type with a rainforest understorey and is dominated by one of the best stands of New England blackbutt trees in the area. One magnificent old blackbutt tree, like the one described on the Nightcap Track, is burnt out by fire. This tree is known as the 'walk-in tree', testimony to the resistance of sclerophyll trees to fire.

Two interesting lookouts are located on the rim. The first is where an old leaning blackbutt tree trunk provides a seat from which you can take in the view of the Doon

Doon Valley with the Doughboy Mountain, a resistant rhyolite plug rising from the floor. The Doughboy was the vent that extruded the rhyolite lavas on the southern part of the shield. You can also view Mt Jerusalem on the caldera rim to the east of the Doon Doon Saddle and Springbrook Plateau to the north. The second lookout at the end of the walk, at Pholis Gap, has a more panoramic view of the caldera, including the Mt Warning complex. The lookout is located to the left of the log safety fence on the gap. Look down on the rainforests of Griers Scrub below the cliffs you are standing on, the meaning of the term 'canopy' is clear, vines and epiphytes are tangled profusely through the tree tops in a dense mat. Pholis Gap is located on the Googarna Road so you can either return by road if you have transport or retrace your steps and experience the walk again.

The best way to approach this walk is probably from the Pholis Lookout end. The National Parks pamphlet is easily read in reverse, and you get the harder uphill sections over while you are fresh. The track is well made with steps set into the steeper slopes and should pose no problems for walkers even the very unfit. This walk is an excellent outing for first-time walkers and families with younger children.

The Historic Flying Fox Site

The walk to the Historic Flying Fox Site commences at the end of Googarna Road. This gravelled road, rather steep in places, leaves Newton Drive to the left, approximately 500 metres before the summit of Mt Nardi. It passes Pholis Gap as it follows the rim of the caldera to the west. Two walking tracks lead off into the bush from the end of the road. One walk 2 kilometres long travels down hill towards the south to the cliff tops high above Mulgum Creek. The other, 5 kilometres long, follows the rim westward to the Flying Fox Site. The track climbs Mt Neville, over 900 metres above sea level, then continues along the rim to a point above Kunghur Creek. The Kunghur Creek Sawmill had a licence to log the Nightcap Forest in the 1940s and 1950s. They solved their transport problems by constructing a huge flying fox to lower logs down the scarp rather than truck them the enormous distance by road. The flying fox had cables 1600 metres long making it the largest in the Southern Hemisphere at the time.

Terania Creek

Terania Creek is one of the small radial streams draining the Nightcap Range to the south of the shield. The forest in the upper part of this valley received national prominence in 1979 when it was the scene of bitter conflict between local conservationists and loggers. The loggers proposed to log the sclerophyll forests on the middle slopes in the basin, below the cliffs but above the rainforests. The conservationists were persistent, well organised, and successful, especially after the Forestry Commission's experts recommended against logging on scientific grounds. The success of this campaign not only saved the forests in Terania Creek Basin, but also led to a reassessment of State Government policy on rainforests, and ultimately to the protection of a much larger area with the dedication of the Nightcap National Park in 1983.

To get to Terania Creek proceed north on the Terania Creek Road from the small village of the Channon, north of Lismore. This road is very narrow and most of the surface is gravelled with several creek fords towards the end that are subject to flooding. You are advised to leave the area at once if heavy rain falls, as rising water levels in the creek close the fords to traffic, trapping you in the forest until the water levels fall. The narrowness of the road and its unsuitability for large logging trucks was one of the telling criticisms used by the Terania

Native Forest Action Group in their successful campaign against logging. You will need to pass through a gate before coming to the end of the road. It is most important to leave gates in the condition you find them, when travelling in rural areas. If the gate is closed you must leave it closed, but if you find it opened you should leave it open. Proceed past the Terania Creek Rainforest Nursery to the camping ground at the end of the road.

The camping ground, a converted logging dump, is equipped with pit toilets and picnic tables. There is a large cleared area where you are permitted to camp overnight, but fires are banned. You will need to carry a camp stove and solid fuel, or take a gas primus. A gas light or strong torch will be required for night light. The only water available at the grounds is creek water which is safe to drink throughout the region only if it satisfies two stringent conditions. Firstly the stream must be running vigorously and second there must not be settlement or development upstream from the site where you are drawing your water. When in doubt it is safer to carry water with you. These two conditions are usually met at the Terania Creek camp site. Walking trails to Protestors Falls and into the Terania Creek Forest lead from the camping ground.

Protestors Falls

The walk to Protestors Falls, 1.4 kilometres return, follows a small tributary stream, Waterfall Creek entering from the right, just before crossing the ford at the carpark. This is a very short walk through a grove of bangalow palms beside the bank of the creek. These palms seem to be the result of frequent disturbance in the form of flooding. The track crosses the stream and ascends up a short flight of steps to the plunge pool at the base of the falls. The falls have been created by a hard and thick layer of rhyolite lava underlayed by less resistant basalt. A thin layer of easily eroded tuff separates these two rock bands causing the rhyolite to overhang the basalt rocks below. It is possible to walk behind the falls on the top layer of basalt. Huge blocks of rhyolite fall out of the cliff as erosion below this layer removes their support. The blocks fall into the plunge pool but the enormous hydraulic force of the water during floods has lifted these huge rocks from the pool and deposited them around the rim. The pool is a pleasant place to have a swim to cool off on a hot day.

Terania Creek Forest walk

The walking trail to the Terania Creek Forest is the abandoned forestry road that continues up the valley from the camping ground. When last walked the track was in a state of dreadful disrepair. The road and its verges were smothered in lantana and crofton weed. The thicket of weeds was so bad in places that it was difficult to force a way through. Near the creeks, where an extra wide lane had been cut in the forest to allow sunlight to penetrate and dry the road, the weeds have grown in lush profusion. Further into the forest, where more sensible practices were employed in the earlier logging, there is sufficient canopy to shade out the weeds and the walking is pleasant. The road must have been a nightmare in the old days as it is a very slippery clay and except in the driest weather care will be needed in selecting a footing. In its present condition the walk can only be recommended to the hardier and more determined bushwalker.

The track crosses and re-crosses the creek as it rises steadily up the valley and eventually peters out just below a relatively high plateau dominated by bangalow palm trees in association with very large brush box trees. The creek crossings are on forestry bridges constructed by laying hollow tree trunks in the stream and covering them with a layer of clay. About half-way up the old road a track leads off to the left on a bend in the road at the top of a small ridge. Follow this track down for one of the real pleasures of this walk, a look at (and swim in?) the circle pool. What appears to be a rhyolite or aplite dyke cuts across the creek creating a series of small but deep pools which culminate in a 3-metre drop into quite a large and inviting pool. This is an excellent place for a lunch stop and if the track were more easily negotiable the walk would be well worthwhile just for a swim in the pools on a hot day. The water in the pools is clear and pleasant to drink, and the sloping rocks on the edge make dry sunny seats.

Much of the rainforest on the lower slopes of the basin has been logged in the past especially during World War II when coachwood was eagerly sought for aircraft construction. Most of the rainforest is dominated by palm glades where it is reasonable to expect that mature rainforest should be growing, suggesting some major disturbance by either wind or fire in the past. The rainforest gives way to sclerophyll forests as you proceed up slope. Large brush box and New England blackbutts grow beneath the cliff line. These were the trees that the loggers eagerly sought but expert advice recommended against felling them, as their great height would make it difficult to fell them on steep slopes without damaging the rainforests below. Some of the brush box trees have been carbon dated from 1200 to 1500 years old.

There are two significant historic sites in the Terania Creek Basin. An Aboriginal site has been identified under a rock overhang on the western slope of the ridge on the eastern side of the valley. Archaeological investigation has revealed evidence of Aboriginal occupation of this 'cave'. No steps have been taken to restrict walkers from visiting the site but no excavations should be undertaken. The other interesting site is an old bridle track approximately 80 metres long and less than 1 metre wide. This track is called 'Gracie's Mistake'. It was proposed to construct an alternate route to the

Nightcap Track over a lower saddle in the Nightcap Range. The saddle chosen was between Dunoon and Rolands Creek, east of the Terania Creek Basin. Unfortunately Mr Grace, the government surveyor at the time, was occupied with office work in Murwillumbah when his roading gang commenced work. Eighty metres of track beginning and ending in the scrub were completed before Mr Grace was aware that his gang were working in the wrong valley, hence the name.

You can also walk up Mackays Road which turns off to the right of Terania Creek Road, just before reaching the camping ground. This road is not trafficable but leads up to the Gibbergunyah Range Road and to the Nightcap Track to the east of Terania Creek. It was proposed at one stage to use this road, instead of the Terania Creek Road, to haul logs out of the basin. Investigation however proved that it was less suitable than the Terania Creek Road, and it is now closed because of a damaged bridge.

Minyon Falls

Three major falls over rhyolite cliffs occur on the southern edge of the caldera remnants. Minyon Falls, Protestors Falls, and Tuntable Falls, all match the Lamington and Springbrook waterfalls for their sheer majestic beauty. Each crashes off the basalt plateau top to plunge 100 metres or so to a plunge pool carved out of the underlying basalt. Each is made more spectacular by the erosion of a tuff and basalt underlay that encourages the rhyolite to break away in large vertical chunks, leaving sheer cliffs behind.

Minyon Falls lies in the hills at the back of Mullumbimby. Most road maps show its location and once in the general area road signs direct you to the top of the falls. The area is maintained by the Forestry Commission of NSW and picnic facilities, barbeques, toilets, and drinking water are provided. If you wish to stay overnight there is a pleasant little camping area maintained by the NSW Forestry Commission at Rummery Park, not far from the falls. Pit toilets, cold showers, and a cooking galley are provided, and a well-designed campfire pit which is much appreciated on those clear cold winter evenings.

The walk to the falls is a circuit but it is preferable to walk in a clockwise direction beginning at the falls. This leaves the most interesting part of the walk until last. From the falls walk or drive the 2 kilometres to the Minyon Grass Picnic Area. The walk begins here and drops down rapidly through dry sclerophyll forest with patches of rainforest in the damper gullies until you reach the plunge pool at the base of the falls. At this point you are almost directly under the lookout at the top of the falls and the walls are so steep that you may actually be in danger if anyone is foolish enough to throw a stone off the top lookout. It is possible to walk around under the falls if you do not mind a drenching but it is not recommended and no track is provided. The plunge pool below the falls looks inviting but beware it is very cold even in the hottest of weather.

After crossing the creek the walk begins to climb the southern escarpment. Along the flatter sections there are some very beautiful sections of forest, with palm glades, red cedars, and some truly magnificent figs. The track then begins to climb steadily up through box forest to the blackbutt forest of the rim. The lush rainforest of the valley floor is a result of the damp sheltered conditions of the gorge and the rich basalt soils derived from the basalts underlying the rhyolite. On the valley sides the poorer rhyolite soils will only support sclerophyll-type forests.

Near the top of the gorge a track branches off to Quandong Falls. These are smaller and can only be viewed from the top but the area makes an excellent lunch stop. On your way back to the main picnic area you will pass through a tea-tree heath association with

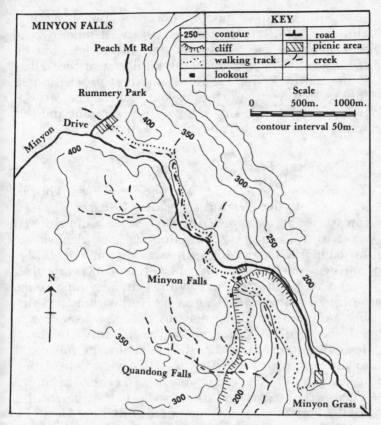

Fig. 19 Track map of walks in the Minyon Falls Area
(Adapted from the 1:25,000 Huonbrook sheet)

some fairly large New England blackbutts and other trees typical of the area. Be on the alert for a small fenced lookout. This gives a grand view of the falls and the whole upper gorge area. Back at the falls there is a viewing platform that gives a spectacular view of the gorge in the area you have just walked through. About half-way back to your car at Minyon Grass there is another lookout that gives a good view of the falls from a different angle.

The round trip is about 9 kilometres and you should allow three to four hours to give yourself time to stop and marvel at the beauty not only of the falls but of the vegetation, particularly the rainforest of the valley floor, and the transition from rainforest to sclerophyll forest. Take your lunch and your camera and wear a pair of comfortable shoes, the walk is pleasant and the tracks are well formed and mostly well graded.

The Nightcap Track

The historic Nightcap Track is one of the better known features of the Nightcap National Park. It was constructed in the pioneering days, when a more direct route from Lismore to Murwillumbah and then on to Brisbane was sought. The only way that mail could be sent between Lismore and Murwillumbah, before this track was constructed, was by the extremely long route down river and along the beaches. Joshua Bray was the first postmaster and the remains of his post office can still be seen at Kynnumboon, near Murwillumbah. Joshua's problem was that the mail ships did not come to the Tweed on a regular basis. To get his mail out it had to go to the more regularly used port at Lismore. There were no overland routes so Joshua employed the local Aborigines to carry the mail to Ballina. However a major problem with this scheme was that the local Murwillumbah tribe did not get along with the neighbouring coastal tribes. Poor Joshua had to row to Tweed Heads and get the Minjungbal people to go down to Ballina. Their relations with tribes to the south seem to have been much better.

It was known that Aborigines frequently crossed the Nightcap Range by reasonably direct routes. Eventually a fairly direct route was constructed through the Doon Doon Saddle linking Murwillumbah to Lismore via Uki. It used to take the mail three days to reach Murwillumbah from Lismore over this difficult track, a trip over and back being a full week's work by the mailman. The second day was spent crossing the remote, lonely and difficult Nightcap Range. This steep rainforest track taxed the energy of the mailman in cyclonic weather when many trees could be expected to be down making the track hazardous. The Nightcap Track was only a bridle track, and a proper road was never built, because a much easier route was eventually surveyed over the Burringbar Range, the location of the present Pacific Highway. Local roads have completed all but 4 kilometres of the Nightcap Track, the last remaining part being the track over the saddle above Doon Doon, the subject of this walk.

The remaining part of this track today links the Gibbergunyah Range Road with the Nightcap Road from Doon Doon. It can be walked in either direction, or for ease of transport can be walked both ways, requiring approximately one-and-a-half hours in each direction. This description is from the Murwillumbah end. The track commences from the hairpin bend at the top of the saddle on the Nightcap Road. This bend can be approached from either Doon Doon in the Tweed Valley or from Huonbrook in the Richmond Valley. A good road map or the very useful Casino State Forests map from the NSW Forestry Commission will help you find your way. The road is usually in good condition but is rather steep especially on the Huonbrook side and a four-wheel drive vehicle is recommended in wet weather. The track follows the rim to the west and the border of the National Park, out of sight from the road, is but a few metres away. The track commences in rainforest but soon gives way to tea-tree heath on poor rhyolitic soils. Three interesting lookouts are located on the rim in this section. The first overlooks Huonbrook towards the south including a magnificent view of Byron Bay. The second gives a spectacular view of the Tweed Valley overlooking the Doughboy Mountain, a resistant acid volcanic plug, and Mt Warning. The third lookout is the best as it looks in both directions combining the views of both previous lookouts. This is a good place to enjoy that cup of tea flavoured with lemon by the leaves of the lemon-scented tea-tree.

There is a junction in the track at this point, the right fork taking you along the rim to Mt Matheson and the left along the Nightcap Track. Take the left fork. The track now turns south and heads towards the Gibbergunyah Range Road. The track is now in rainforest on rich soils on the Blue Knob basalt lava flows. Look for the large old New England blackbutt trees on your left, their butts typically blackened by fires in the past. One of these trees is hollow and if you climb inside you will be amazed at the size of the hollow. Blackbutts often seem to have a large 'pipe' and in this tree successive fires over the years have enlarged the pipe so that all that remains of the living tree is a thin skirt of growth wood with very little means of support. Not long after passing the blackbutts you will walk through an interesting patch of small rainforest. Many of the trees have been named and there is a moderately sized red cedar and two trees marked during the original survey.

Just before reaching the Gibbergunyah Range Road the soil becomes poorer as acid volcanic rocks are again encountered. This part of the track is lined with a dry type of rainforest with smaller trees and a heath-like understorey. The somewhat damper southerly aspect probably assists rainforest in this location in which it is more likely to expect sclerophyll forest. The southern entrance to the track is well signposted and protected from trail bike riders by a fence and gate. The Nightcap Track is relatively flat and is suitable for walkers of all ages.

The old Nightcap Track made its contribution to history and then faded away as the coastal settlements grew and the roads were extended along the flatter coastal route. It was never used for heavy transport and the unreliability of early motor vehicles precluded its use

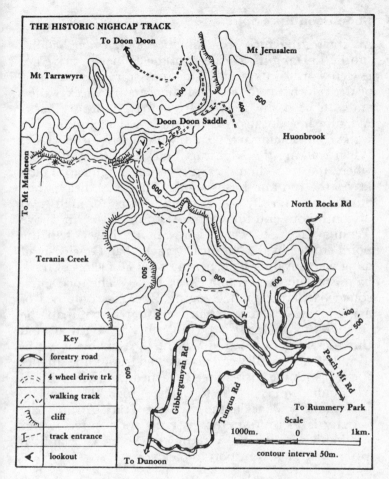

THE HISTORIC NIGHCAP TRACK

To Doon Doon

Mt Tarrawyra

Mt Jerusalem

Doon Doon Saddle

Huonbrook

To Mt Matheson

North Rocks Rd

Terania Creek

Gibbergunyah Rd

Tungun Rd

Peach Mt Rd

To Rummery Park

Key	
	forestry road
	4 wheel drive trk
	walking track
	cliff
	track entrance
	lookout

To Dunoon

Scale

1000m.   0   1km.

contour interval 50m.

*Fig. 20 Track map of the Historic Nightcap Track
(Adapted from the 1:25,000 Huonbrook sheet)*

or development as a major direct road link between the
two valleys. The pinches were too steep, the track was
too narrow, and the surface too rough to allow heavy
drays or the early motor vehicles to negotiate it with
safety.

Doon Doon Rock Spire

An interesting rock spire on the Doon Doon Saddle, similar to Hanging Rock east of the Tomewin tick gate, is well worth walking to. This rock spire is on the rim of the caldera, at the head of the Terania Creek Valley and can be easily reached from the Nightcap Track. Actually it is located on the track system linking the walks commencing at Mt Nardi with the Nightcap Track. When walking the Nightcap Track take the right fork where the track branches just as the Nightcap Track leaves the rim and heads south. This track heads west along the rim by zig-zagging down through two discontinuous cliff lines to a low point on the rim above Terania Creek. It was this low point, lower than the point crossed by the Nightcap Track, that 'Gracies' road gang were heading for when they cut 80 metres of track by mistake in the Terania Creek Valley. The rock spire, somewhat larger than Hanging Rock, is composed of agglomerate and has resisted erosion better than the surrounding rocks. It is possible to walk right around this rock to get a good view of it. Reasonable views of Terania Creek Valley can also be had from some smaller rocks before the rock spire is reached, but it is a bit of a scramble to get to the top. These rocks are easier to find on the way back to the Nightcap Track. An alternate activity is to continue on past the rock spire towards Mt Matheson and the walking tracks of Mt Nardi, if you can arrange transport to pick you up.

The Big Scrub Flora Reserve

The 'big scrub' was the title given by the cedar-cutters, to the extensive lowland rainforest that covered the basalt-capped hills north of Lismore. This subtropical rainforest of the white booyong type contained the best and most extensive stands of red cedar trees in New South Wales and was a cedar-cutter's paradise. Unfortunately the pioneering farmers who followed the cedar-cutters also considered this land, with its fertile red volcanic soil, a paradise. Their paradise however involved dairy cows and had precious little room for trees, so most of the 'Big Scrub' disappeared under the settlers' axes. The cedar-cutters may have 'raped' the cedar trees but the farmers certainly 'raped' the 'Big Scrub'! The Big Scrub Flora Reserve is the only substantial remaining stand left in the Richmond Valley and it is certainly worth visiting.

The Big Scrub Flora Reserve is easily visited when walking the historic Nightcap Track as it is located at the lower end of the Gibbergunyah Range Road near Rocky Lake, Lismore's water supply. You can easily drive down the Gibbergunyah Range Road from the Lismore end of the Nightcap Track. If this reserve is approached from the Lismore end and you have no intention of visiting the Nightcap Track you will be able to drive to the reserve in a conventional vehicle even in wet weather. Two short walking circuits have been constructed on the eastern side of the road. The lower one is only about half as long as the upper track and leaves you plenty of time to enjoy the majestic trees and the melodies of the birds.

Park your vehicle at the sign indicating the walking track and enjoy one of the best examples of rainforest anywhere in the world. It will take you about one hour to stroll along the relatively level circular track. Many trees have been labelled for your information. Touch the smooth bark of the small but fascinating python tree and feel its coolness. Notice the half-eaten black and crab apples lying on the ground, discarded by possums. If you arrive early in the day listen to the profusion of bird life feeding on the abundant fruits of the trees. The best time to take one of these walks is in the early morning when the birds are singing their territorial chorale. You will be amazed at the variety of calls heard within a few minutes of entering the forest. Green, brown and flock pigeons, catbirds and whipbirds to name but a few sing the glories of life and an eloquent condemnation of the forestry practice of clear felling. The planted stands of blackbutt and flooded gum seem almost deserted compared with the incredible variety of bird life found in this forest.

These few remaining stands of lowland forest are a vital link in the chain of a continuous food supply for fruitivorous birds in the region. If you are reasonably quiet you will hear the bounds of wallabies as they carefully remain ahead of you but out of view. You may be extremely fortunate and see one of these but our attempts to spotlight these with a torch at night has failed even though they could be clearly heard nearby. This forest is an excellent place to escape the pressures of modern living.

Interestingly one tree that was a native of this specific area is making a strong comeback in the nearby hills. The Macadamia nut tree is being grown in thousands in the immediate vicinity in what promises to be a very profitable agricultural enterprise. The Macadamia is one of the few native plants to be grown commercially. A sad comment on the attitude to the native plants of the early settlers is the fact that the use of the Macadamia as a commercial tree crop was developed in Hawaii. The gentleman responsible for their name and their growth commercially was the Macadam well known for his development of the technique of road building (macadamised roads) which has become the standard for modern road construction.

PART III
BUSHCRAFT

10
Bushcraft

From the inception of the colony of New South Wales white Australians have had a deep fear and distrust of the bush. Early settlers from English cities and towns huddled on the shores of Port Jackson and for many years hardly ventured beyond sight of the convict settlement. Later the poetry and stories of Banjo Paterson and Henry Lawson lauded the qualities of the pioneers of the bush and the general population raised them to the stature of heroes and made heroic epics out of their simple struggles. Today the largely urban Australian society, while giving lip-service to environmental issues and the bush tradition, energetically avoids contact with the environment. However there are signs this is changing. Many more people are venturing into the bush and the prominence given to environmental issues is awakening people's curiosity and courage to 'go bush'. The bush holds few terrors and all can be overcome with the right equipment, the right maps, the right attitude, and an understanding of the conditions pertaining to that area.

Equipment

Most of the bushwalks described in this book can be completed with a bare minimum of equipment. However a little of the right equipment can make your walking much more enjoyable. And this depends on the type of walk you are attempting, your age, and the size of your bank balance. The young may trip through the bush in thongs and a T-shirt and happily sleep under the stars. If you are one of those skip this section.

Day walks
Even a short ramble through the scrub can be most unpleasant for the unprepared. The prudent take with them some or all of the following:

Comfortable walking **shoes** which need not be expensive hiking boots, joggers will do. Rainforest tracks have a habit of discovering the weaknesses in footwear, and while joggers are light and usually comfortable, they are not waterproof. Remember you are walking in rainforest, and something made of leather will remain dry. One friend of ours swears by Wellington boots but you need not go to this extreme. If you are spending money on boots look for those with waterproofed tongues.

Socks are in contact with your skin so look for the best quality you can afford. Army surplus socks are cheap and they will give you some protection against leeches, as well as being comfortable and providing a means of avoiding blisters. Avoid open weave socks such as walk socks or football socks, leeches penetrate the open weave easily.

Take a **raincoat** or some form of **waterproof clothing**, avoiding plastics as the condensation of your sweat is just as wet as the rain outside. Nylon sprayjackets when new will give you some protection against rain and will also prevent wind chill and body-heat loss if you are cold. They do suffer from condensation so if you can afford it get yourself a coat made out of a material that has the capacity to breathe. Japara cotton is the best cloth available for this purpose and can be made quite waterproof. A newer synthetic cloth called Gortex claims to have all the characteristics of Japara and appears to be superior but is a more expensive alternative. When you look at the design make sure it has adequate ventilation and that it can be opened down the front to allow you to adjust the internal temperature under hot steamy conditions. Remember that even though it is not actually raining at the time you are walking you will still be soaked from your contact with wet vegetation.

A **water bottle** is a useful appendage as most of the easier routes are along the ridge tops where water is not available. Even in heavy rain you may not be able to obtain water without a long scramble down to the lower reaches of a creek. Creek water is safe to drink only when the creek is flowing vigorously and there is no habitation or development upstream.

Clothing should be comfortable and appropriate to the conditions. Long pants and a long-sleeved top may protect you from wait-a-whiles and thorn bushes, but you will soon become adept at avoiding them, experience is a great teacher. Shorts are more comfortable in wet weather unless it is mid-winter.

Maps are generally unnecessary on this type of walk but can be very instructive. The guided walk notes provided by the National Parks can be very useful and aid immeasurably your understanding and enjoyment of the environment.

A bush **hat** to protect your face is often very useful.

If you like a cup of tea or coffee a small **solid fuel stove** is useful. solid fuel or hexamine stoves use small fuel pellets, they are small, light, and effective when not exposed to wind. It is very difficult to get dry firewood in the rainforest and a fire can take you two to three hours to establish. Additionally the National Parks people do not like fires being used, particularly in the forest margins where thoughtlessness can create a considerable disaster if fire gets away. Carry your matches in a waterproof container, even so-called waterproof matches are of little use when sodden. Usually both matches and stove can be stowed safely in your billy.

A light **day pack** to carry your camera, lunch and surplus gear makes life a lot easier. Pack all your gear inside plastic bags in your pack. Even the waterproof packs will leak from the continual rubbing against your back as you walk.

If you intend to take photographs you will need either a flash or a tripod. Exposure times in the rainforest are long because of the limited light even at midday.

Overnight walks

Walks where you are expecting to camp out overnight require much the same equipment as mentioned above with some additional items.

You will need a **tent** which need not be a major expense as the light nylon tent is quite cheap and can be very effective accommodation. Tents with sidewalls are generally more comfortable than those without and the extra weight is well justified in a storm or heavy rain. Make sure the tent is well ventilated and can be ventilated even in the heaviest rain otherwise the condensation inside the tent will soak you. The average person breathes out about a pint of water during a night and it will condense on your tent walls and run down on to the floor. Most tents now have sewn-in floors which not only protect you from insects and the animal life but also provide you with some insulation against heat loss to the ground.

The most important thing to have with a nylon tent is a good fly. With a fly even in the heaviest rain you will be snug and dry. Heavy rain goes straight through nylon and is merely broken into a fine mist. The fly will slow down the rain in this manner and your tent will protect you and your possessions. Additionally the eaves of the fly give you somewhere to stow packs and other bulky and awkward items. When buying a fly look carefully at getting one a size too big for your tent. Usually it will still fit length-wise but will give you the option of pegging it straight into the ground or using the overhang for secondary storage.

There are some excellent tents on the market but they

are very expensive. The nylon tents are so effective that you are buying lightness and portability so be sure that you really are getting a significant reduction in weight.

Backpacks There are many styles of backpack on the market, varying greatly in price. You should look for certain attributes given the environment you are entering.

There should be no protruding parts to catch on the vegetation. The backpack should not ride too high on your back as it will catch on the many branches and limbs you will have to scramble under.

Since you must carry a fairly large amount of gear the backpack should have a reasonable capacity and some method of distributing the weight from your shoulders. This is usually accomplished by a frame or a flexible pad of some kind. Internal frames are less likely to catch on the vegetation and bring you to sudden and unexpected stops.

A waist strap can be used to take the weight off your shoulders, but should be easily detachable to allow you to duck under logs and other obstacles and to give you the flexibility to climb if necessary. Waterproofing would be desirable but it is usually not effective so it is sensible to pack your gear in plastic bags.

Sleeping bags A sleeping bag is an essential for overnight camping. The range of styles and prices is very broad, but a few considerations related to the local environment will help to narrow the choice.

Winters can be very cold in the rainforests of the higher ridges, so warmth must be a consideration. However summer nights are warm and a very warm bag is not necessary. The solution to this problem could be to buy two bags or a good quality down sleeping bag. Either of these alternatives can be quite expensive and there is a cheaper alternative. The camp-quilt style of bag allows you to close it right up in cold weather and open it up when the weather is warm. The one bag can be made to suit both weather conditions. In general the 'mummy' or hooded types of bag cannot attain the versatility of the camp-quilts.

The bag you choose should perform well in wet conditions. This eliminates down bags as they lose most of their insulating qualities when wet. The cheaper synthetic linings especially Dacron Hollofill have good insulation qualities and will perform reasonably even when wet. Their main problem is their bulkiness and their inability to be compressed into the space available in most packs.

The fill in a sleeping bag performs the function of separating the outer and inner linings and maintaining a layer of insulating air between them. Some bags are sewn right through and let your body heat out through the stitching. Moderately expensive bags avoid this problem by using a double layer of fill which is stitched separately.

Forget about any maker's claims about showerproofing or waterproofing, if you want a good night's sleep you will pack your sleeping bag inside a plastic garbage bag before stowing it in its stuff bag. This is the only way to keep your bag dry in the rainforest. (The stuff bag over the plastic bag helps to prevent the plastic from being punctured or torn by twigs and thorns.)

A sign of a better quality bag is an anti-draft flap to cover the zipper and prevent heat loss. Of course when you lay one of these bags out you make sure that the side with the flap is uppermost so that it naturally falls down over the zipper.

Air beds or sleeping mats The major heat loss you are likely to incur is heat loss to the ground. This is overcome partly in some sleeping bags by having a thicker lining on the bottom, but your weight will still compress the fill and allow heat loss. This is especially so in rainforest where you are most likely to be sleeping on damp ground where conduction of body heat is at its greatest. The alternative to a cold night is to carry some form of insulation. Air beds will do the job but are either very heavy or very fragile.

The modern alternative is the closed-cell foam sleeping mat. This provides excellent insulation and helps to take the hardness off the ground on which you are sleeping. It is cheap, light, water resistant, and an excellent investment since it ensures a warm and comfortable night's sleep to refresh you for another day's hiking. The self-inflating air bed is light and very compact but expensive and have yet to prove its value, but are worth a try if you can afford one.

Dry clothes You are in a rainforest and you must expect to be wet so dry clothes to sleep in are essential. These should always be packed inside a plastic bag. The plastic bag can be effectively sealed by putting a few twists in the neck and placing it in your pack upside down.

Food If you are undertaking strenuous activity you will need sustaining food. There are several problems in this area since water for cooking and cleaning must all be carried if you camp on the ridge tops. Canned food is very heavy and you must carry the cans out with you. The old idea of burn, bash, and bury no longer applies as the numbers of people using the rainforests would soon see the whole area underlain by a layer of steel from buried cans. Dehydrated foods are light but rather expensive and bland to the taste.

The better alternative is some vegetables such as broccoli, carrots, peas and beans, combined with say instant mashed potatoes for some bulk. A little bacon or devon will keep for a few days and can be fried up to add a little interest to your meals. Meat can also be cut thinly and dried out in a microwave oven to add to your meals. This is not only the cheapest type of meal but it is also very light and is good for you. Eggs can be carried packed in your billy to add some extra protein to your diet. Dried fruits will give you something to munch along the track as well as maintain your regularity. Speaking of regularity you should always remember to carry some toilet paper packed in a plastic bag. Soggy toilet paper is a real disaster as the only large leaves you are likely to find are the leaves of the Queensland stinging tree.

First aid A good first-aid kit is needed but you can treat most injuries with a few basic essentials. A roll of elastoplast dressing strip will provide you with bandaids for minor cuts and scratches as well as binding up sprains and even acting as a fixative for a splint should you be so unlucky as to require one. Some aspirin and some disinfectant cream complete a kit that will allow you to treat most of the minor injuries that are likely. Salt works in removing leeches but is a destructive method. Simply grasping the leech and removing it is quicker, and certainly better for the leech.

Camping out of a car

When camping out of a car you can increase the amount of gear you can take. A gas cooker is a useful item which will save you time spent trying to get a fire for a cup of tea. Another useful item often overlooked is a comfortable collapsible chair which can make it possible to relax and rest your weary back even when the ground is very wet. A gas light and some reading material will help to pass the long hours between sundown and your usual bedtime.

Consideration may be given to taking the ingredients of a bush damper. Self-raising flour, drinking water, milk powder, and salt is all that is needed, though a little cream will produce a very tasty and professional product. The old days of cinder exteriors for dampers have passed and a roll of aluminium foil can provide you with an inexpensive camp oven. When you roll the mixture up in the foil make sure you leave enough space for the damper to rise or it will burst out into the coals. Make a long thin damper, it will cook more rapidly and will suffer a minimum of charring. Another alternative is 'twisties', not the commercial kind but damper mixture coiled around a dry stick and toasted in the fire. Finish both off with butter and 'Cockies Joy' (Golden Syrup for the uninitiated).

Navigation

The most embarrassing situation that can occur to you when you are bushwalking, is to become lost and be the subject of an organised search party. This can be avoided with a little preparation, the right equipment, and some basic navigation skills. We hope that this book will help you find your way in this region, but you will require more than this on some of the walks.

Basic navigation equipment for walkers is a compass and the right maps. A compass can give some walkers a false sense of security because a compass is only useful to a walker with an appropriate map and knowledge of your position on the map. Compasses are only useful to help you read your map. There are many different types of maps and different maps are required for different walks. One other essential thing all walking parties should do is to inform someone of where they intend to go and give a reasonable indication of when they expect to return. This information must be reasonably reliable and requires that some detailed planning is done before you leave. If the information is not reasonably accurate you may find that search parties are out looking for you when you are not lost. This has the potential to be more embarrassing than really being lost.

One other important consideration is the size of your party and the way the party is managed on the track. We consider that the minimum safe size on the more difficult walks is four walkers. In the event of a serious injury one can remain with the patient while the other two go for help. Walking unaccompanied is not recommended at the best of times but one person rushing for help is a recipe for disaster. When walking with large parties it is important to keep the party together. If the party gets separated there is danger that one part of it will get lost. It is very difficult to get your party back together when this happens as each group is not aware what the other groups are doing. The speed of a walking party is therefore the speed of the slowest member. Two of the more experienced members should both lead a large group and bring up the rear, especially when novice walkers are included in your group. The leaders should be responsible for keeping the party together. The party should be regrouped at each point where there is some danger of members getting lost. Such places are usually junctions in the track system and places where trails make abrupt changes in direction, are obstructed by fallen trees or are otherwise indistinct. It is a good rule to regroup your party at every track intersection or other significant point.

Maps

The type of maps required varies from walk to walk. Graded tracks require different maps to trails and wilderness areas. The one constant map that you will need is a local road map. There are many of these and local road maps can be supplied by the tourist authorities in the area, or you may be able to get one from your motoring organisation. Other bodies often have good maps available. The 'Casino Project Map' produced by the Forestry Commission for the Casino and Coffs Harbour Forestry Districts is a good basic map for the southern half of the region and for areas to the south and west. This map is available at forestry offices throughout the region. A good road map should show all of the roads in the area, not just the main ones as quite a few walks commence from infrequently used roads. A good local road map will ensure that you can find the start of all of the walks listed in this book with a minimum of fuss. It will, more importantly, assist people who are helping you with transport when you are walking from one point to another, to find you efficiently at the end of your trip.

Simple tracks and circuits

Some tracks do not require maps at all. These are walking tracks that are clearly made and signposted and do not have intersecting tracks running off them. The track to the summit of Mt Warning is one of these. You must not stray off these tracks or take short cuts. Apart from damaging the ecosystem unnecessarily, you run the danger of getting lost. Walkers have often been lost on Mt Warning because of taking short cuts. Much of the Mt Warning track zig-zags up a steep slope. Walkers have sometimes been keen to reduce the distance walked by short-cutting straight down the slope as they return. They usually get into difficulties on the last leg as their short cut leads them to Cedar Creek, there being no track below. However carrying the track map in the information pamphlet supplied by the National Parks and Wildlife Service adds considerable interest to the trip, as well as being a valued souvenir. These pamphlets are usually available at information posts at the entrances to most of the National Parks in the region. They can also be obtained from the offices of that organisation.

Graded track systems

It is essential to carry a track map when walking on graded track networks as in the Lamington National Park. These maps are available from the rangers of the National Parks and they can often be obtained from the kiosks at Binna Burra and O'Reillys. Track maps are used in the same way that you would use a road map. You need to read the signposts on the track system carefully and consult your map at each intersection. You can easily keep track of your location on the map by making use of all of the available landmarks shown on the map. These usually include track intersections, distance markers, creek crossings, lookouts, rest areas, and special points of interest. Some frequently used tracks have detailed guides prepared for them. The guided walks are useful, not just for showing you the way, but because of the information about the environment they impart. These tracks are set up with clearly marked stopping-points with short notes explaining the specific feature at that point. Self-guided walks are recommended as an excellent starting-point for those new to the environment who wish to acquire knowledge rapidly. Other more detailed maps sometimes also show the track networks. The Queensland Forestry has an excellent large-scale map of the Lamington with all of the tracks and trails marked clearly in red. We have found this map so useful that we bought a second copy when the first one disintegrated. Topographic maps, particularly ones with larger scales often have the tracks and trails marked on them. These are available from the two State Mapping Authorities (remember you are in a border area), additionally relevant copies are often stocked by tourist information centres and local newsagents.

Blazed trails and wilderness areas

When Bernard O'Reilly set out in search of the Stinson airliner on that February day in 1937 he travelled light, but there was one item that he was very careful to pack in his sugar bag. He took with him the very latest and best map of the McPherson Ranges that he could obtain. He consulted this map constantly to keep track of his position. On discovering two survivors after two days of searching he consulted his map for the last time. He ascertained the precise position of the wreck and chose the quickest route to civilisation and help for the injured. He chose to walk straight down Christmas Creek, then threw the cloth-backed map to Joe Binsted to use as protection from the rain that was sure to fall again that night. If Bernard O'Reilly, an experienced bushman, with knowledge of the area needed to take a map then so do you.

You should carry large-scale maps when you are walking on blazed trails and especially if you intend to enter the wilderness. Topographic maps or maps produced by the forestry or National Parks are recommended. It is best to choose a map with the trail marked on it if one is available. We are currently using the 1:25,000 scale topographic maps which are proving to be ideal because of their large scale and because many of the trails are marked on them. Their one disadvantage is the large size and the fact that you need so many to cover a large area. We were forced to take three maps to gain an adequate coverage of the Washpool National Park on a recent trip. These topographic maps are readily available, for both sides of the border, at the Murwillumbah Information Centre and are of course available from the mapping authorities of both States.

Topographic maps show a lot of detail but the dominant feature on them is the contour lines. These lines, usually printed in brown, show altitude in the same way that the lines on a weather map show air pressure. With practice it is easy to recognise individual peaks, ridges, valleys, plains and other features on the map. When walking on trails these peaks, ridges and valleys act as landmarks that can be recognised both on the map and on the trail. Other features such as creeks and many others act as additional landmarks that can be used to confirm your location. With a bit of experience with a map in the field you will soon become expert at finding your way.

Trails are different to tracks in that a made footpath has not been constructed. Trails are rarely graded and frequently travel straight up slope, so are often considerably steeper than tracks. This difficulty is compensated for, to some extent, by the shorter distance between two points by the more direct route. Old trails were marked by blazing trees along the way. These blazes were small nicks cut in the bark of trees by an axe or machete, usually at between waist and shoulder height. Modern trail markers are bits of brightly coloured tape tied to trees. These have two advantages. They do not harm the vegetation and they can easily be removed if they are wrongly placed. Blazes cut with an axe are permanent and cannot be erased if cut in error. Indiscriminate blazing in the past has caused many problems in some areas. You should take great care to follow the blazes and must stop as soon as you are aware that you have lost the trail. It is futile to continue on, charging through the scrub in the hope of regaining the trail at some point ahead. Trails can often be very difficult to find in the bush. The correct procedure is to go back to where you last saw a blaze and carefully find where the track goes from that point. The most frequent places where you will lose the trail is where an abrupt change in direction is made or the trail is obscured by fallen trees or undergrowth. To lose the trail occasionally is often unavoidable, but it is a different thing altogether to get lost. You will not get lost if you consult the map regularly as you pass each landmark that can be identified on both the trail and the map. When walking along the Border Track in the Lamington you can count off on the map, the individual peaks crossed by the trail. Other strategies will suggest themselves if you study the map regularly in different types of terrain.

Using a compass

A compass is not often required when travelling along trails, especially when following the rim of the caldera. However you should carry one in case of emergencies. It is sometimes useful for checking your direction and confirming your position on the map. Do not believe the old bush folk lore, that claims that you can check your direction by the moss growing on the southern side of tree trunks. The only trees with which we can do this with any certainty are those with a flaky bark such as the red cedar. These trees are rare in rainforests as most trees have a relatively fine-textured bark that is grey in appearance.

Compasses can be used to orient maps in the field.

To do this, place your map on the ground and put your compass on it. Rotate the map until the north arrow on the map is parallel to the compass needle. A correctly oriented map is much easier to read when used in the field. A compass can sometimes be used to take a back bearing from some prominent feature. We have not found it necessary to do this when walking in the Tweed region. Taking back bearings requires some skill and experience. Additionally you will have to carry a pencil, ruler, and protractor to mark this bearing on your map. You should carry a compass but you may not have much use for it in this terrain, as generally a compass is required in flatter, featureless country. We have found the use of a compass necessary when walking in the wilderness of Stotts Island on a cloudy day.

Navigating in the bush is not difficult. A little preparation studying your maps before the trip can help a great deal. You will only acquire experience in using maps in the field by consulting them regularly. Why not become the navigator in your party and sharpen up your map-reading skills? With good maps, some practice, and some commonsense you can ensure that you do not get lost.

Caring for an endangered system

The forests and fauna of the Tweed volcano are among the most beautiful and rarest in the world. Properly maintained and properly promoted they represent a resource that the people of the Tweed may use for all the foreseeable future. The responsibility for the maintenance of this unique area rests as much with you as with the relevant government departments.

When we make use of the bush we need to remember that there are certain rules of good manners that apply in much the same way as those we observe when visiting a friend's home. These rules of behaviour are changing as the wilderness areas come to be used by more and more people. Overseas you occasionally have to queue up to get into a national park and there is no reason why a similar situation should not develop here. In the past our use of these resources has been relatively free and easy. Given the pressure that they are already receiving and the likelihood of that pressure increasing we can no longer enjoy the unrestricted enjoyment of our wilderness.

Here are some basic rules we must follow to care for a rare and beautiful environment. The observance of these simple rules will help to stall off the day when our freedom to use national parks will be restricted.

Leave it as you find it. You have enjoyed a unique experience.
Do not take that opportunity away from others. Here are some specific **do's and don'ts**.

Do not remove things from the forest No matter how much you crave that pretty little rock orchid remember that you are only one of many thousands visiting the forest. If each visitor took one tiny little plant the area would be stripped clean within a very short period of time.

Take out what you bring in Everything should be carried out, even biodegradable items, and deposited in the nearest litter bin. Paper, plastics, and tins are the main items in this category. They will decompose eventually but by then they will be underneath the next layer of litter dropped by the irresponsible. Do not bury tins, the area would soon be paved in steel underneath the most favoured camp sites. Do not burn plastics, they give off highly toxic gases that are bad for you as well as the environment.

Biodegradable items such as orange peels and apple cores should be buried if they must be left behind, but it is usually less bother to carry them out and certainly is the best course of action.

Do not use detergents to wash up Detergents foul the water supply and have a harmful effect on the wildlife.

Take a hand full of gravel instead, it will clean down most cooking utensils and have no harmful effects.

Choose toilet areas carefully On several occasions we have come across a nice camp site only to find it littered with suspicious squares of white paper. Please choose a spot well away from the track or camp site and do bury your doings.

Resist the urge to clear room for your camp site Favoured areas can rapidly become depressing mud heaps as the ground cover is steadily pushed further and further back by successive groups of campers who just make a little extra space.

Use existing fireplaces, particularly where they are provided.

Leave your axe at home and save your machete or your bush saw for cutting up dead wood. No one wants to see your name carved in a tree, you will only be embarrassed by it later on.

Keep your noise to a minimum. Too much noise and you will not see any wildlife and destroy the experience for others. Leave your generator and hi-fi equipment at home. You may be surprised how relaxed you will feel without access to the latest news.

Do not **light a fire** in periods of high bushfire danger. This is not only foolish but potentially fatal.

Take care on country roads you use for access. Farm vehicles use them, straying stock, and wildlife are often encountered on them.

Obtain permission to cross private property. Most farmers will be annoyed if you invade their property without the courtesy of asking but most farmers will give you permission and help out with local information if you show the courtesy of asking.

Leave farm gates as you find them. Open if they were open and closed if they were closed.

Do not get lost and do not take unnecessary risks. The cost in time and effort to the volunteers who come to your aid is considerable, as will be your embarrassment.

When in national parks **follow the National Parks' code of behaviour**. In Queensland and New South Wales the essentials are the same.

> Be careful with fire.
> Do not interfere with plants or animals.
> Firearms are prohibited.
> Leave domestic pets at home.
> Do not short-cut graded walking tracks.
> Obtain camping permits in Queensland.
> Do not leave litter.

Whether you seek exercise, achievement, education or solitude the forests of the ancient Tweed volcano will have something for you. Nowhere in Australia is such a beautiful and interesting area so readily accessible. Nowhere in the world are so many rare and endangered species so closely grouped together. The area is an ideal place to study the inter-relationships of nature, to get closer to nature, and to find, in your own way, your roots in this most miraculous and enchanting planet that is our home.

APPENDIX 1
PLACENAMES OF THE TWEED

The placenames of any area provide clues to the history and background of the inhabitants. In old world countries such as Britain and France the origins of the names of places goes back into antiquity, to the very depths of the culture from which they spring. The placenames of the Tweed spring mainly from four sources. The first source is the deep longing of the colonists for their homeland, the best example of this is the Tweed River named after the stream that forms the boundary between England and Scotland. A second more powerful source is the desire of the colonists and explorers to leave their mark on the newly discovered lands, naming prominent features after themselves or other prominent people of the time. A third more subtle source is the names that are applied to places through common usage, names that are descriptive such as The Pinnacle, Point Lookout or Main Arm. The fourth and in many ways more interesting source is the placenames passed down to us from the Aboriginal inhabitants, the Tweed district has a surprising number of placenames derived from this source.

The culture and language of the Aboriginal inhabitants of the Tweed River district disappeared rapidly under the pressure of the white settlers. None of the whites saw fit to attempt to record these elements of Aboriginal society in a detailed and coherent manner. We do know some of their words where they fell into use by whites as placenames. The surveyor Roberts used predominantly Aboriginal names for the main peaks in the McPherson Ranges. Major difficulties have arisen in the interpretation of many of these placenames since the Aboriginal inhabitants had no written language. The spellings recorded by the white settlers depended on how they heard the word used by Aborigines at the time.

Additionally the meaning ascribed to the placenames was subject to confusion and misinterpretation since they were recorded by people who had no knowledge of the intricacies and subtleties of the language. In many cases the Aboriginal names used have no descriptive functions. For example Bithongabel means little trees or scrub, but the mountain is capped by very large trees which are obviously quite ancient and must have been extremely large when Roberts named the mountain.

We know that the language was a dialect of the Bundjalung group of languages used in the valleys to the south but we do not know how the word usage varied from the southern dialects. As a result there is much confusion both in the spellings and the meanings of major placenames. For a full discussion of these aspects readers are recommended to obtain a copy of the authoritative work by the Richmond–Tweed Regional Library. This list confines itself to the most accepted spellings and meanings and omits the more obviously descriptive names.

Bald Mountain: The poor soils from the rhyolite capping on this mountain in the Limpinwood area gave rise to a hill with forested skirts and a thin brush capping so the name is largely descriptive.

Best of all Lookouts: Descriptive term.

Biby: From the Aboriginal word for the white-leaved box tree or the white gum.

Big Scrub (The): Local name for the huge expanse of subtropical rainforest found on the basalt uplands south of Mt Warning.

Binnaburra: (or Binna Burra) Aboriginal word for the place of the beech trees.

Bithongabel (Mount): An Aboriginal name given by the surveyor Roberts meaning little trees or scrub.

Blackbutts (The): A spectacular lookout named for the magnificent New England blackbutt trees found there in a somewhat unusual location surrounded by rainforest.

Blue Knob: Probably a colonist's descriptive term but may come from the Aboriginal for the dark side of the mountain.

Boogarem (Mount): Probably a tongue-in-cheek corruption of a common bullockies' curse. An alternative explanation is that it has some Aboriginal connection meaning mythology or black bean tree.

Border Ranges: Descriptive term since the crest of much of the range delineates the border between NSW and Qld.

Brindle Creek: Named after a wild brindle bullock.

Brummies Lookout: Brummie was a cedar-getter who used this high point to locate valuable cedar trees in the area. During the winter months the cedars lose their leaves and in spring the new growth is a delicate pink shade and the cedars stand out in the forest.

Burrell (Mount): Derived from an Aboriginal name probably meaning wallaby (see Byrill Creek).

Byrill Creek: Probably derived from the Aboriginal word for wallaby.

Cedar Creek: Descriptive term.

Chillingham: May be a transplanted English village

name or derived from the Aboriginal name for the area, said to be Chinningum. Probably a convenient combination of both.

Cominan (Mount): From the Aboriginal for big things or big trees.

Condong; A corruption of the name of the blue fig or brush quandong.

Cougal: Various possible meanings, perhaps from an Aboriginal word meaning big rock.

Dinseys Rock: Named after an early settler, also called Environ Rock.

Doon Doon: From an Aboriginal word meaning grave.

Durigan (Mount): Named by Roberts from an Aboriginal word meaning a lead, guide or landmark.

Echo Point: A recent descriptive name for a point below Mt Cominan from which echoes can be bounced off the slopes of Mt Worendo.

Fingal: From the area of the Giants Causeway, Northern Ireland, which has similar columnar basalt rock formations.

Forest Top: Descriptive term.

Gibbergunyah: Not an Aboriginal word but a corruption and combination of two Aboriginal words gibber, meaning stone, and gunyah, meaning hut or shelter.

Gipps (Mount): Named by the surveyor Roberts after the Governor of NSW, Sir George Gipps.

Gradys Creek: named after a settler.

Green Pigeon: Named for the bird of the same name (*Chalcophaps indica*).

Hanging Rock: Descriptive term also known as Mebbin Rock.

Hobwee (Mount): Named by Roberts the surveyor in 1864 from an Aboriginal word meaning get out. Some confusion as to its location (see note on Mt Merino).

Hopping Dick Creek: Named after settler Dick Wood who hopped because he had a limp (see Limpinwood).

Koonorigan: From the Aboriginal for running water.

Koonyum Range: From the Aboriginal for anus?

Kunghur: Aboriginal for collect or gather.

Kynnumboon: Named by early settler Joshua Bray probably from the Aboriginal for any of the following; roots, open swamp or place of possums. Another less likely meaning is rocks since the area currently called Kynnumboon is in the middle of an alluvial plain.

Kyogle: Probably Aboriginal for scrub turkey.

Limpinwood: From settler Dick Wood who had a limp.

McPherson Range: Named by the explorer Allan Cunningham after a Major Duncan McPherson.

Matheson (Mount): Named after the government surveyor who surveyed the Nightcap Track.

Mayal Creek: Also known as Murdering Creek, site of

the killing of two cedar-getters in 1846 by local Aborigines.

Mebbin: From the Aboriginal for hawk.

Merino (Mount): From an Aboriginal word possibly derived from the word for breasts or wallaby or cloud or alive. Incorrectly located on the 1967 1:50,000 military map which has led to further errors such as the one on the display map at the Blackbutts Lookout. In both cases Mount Hobwee has been confused with Mount Merino.

Midginbil: From the Aboriginal word for the walking stick palm (*Linospadix monostachya*).

Minyon Falls: From either an Aboriginal word for high and dry or from the name of the local Aboriginal tribe the Minyungbal.

Minyon Grass: Numerous places on the Northern Rivers were referred to as grasses, probably because the existence of grass at any point within the forest was a valuable piece of information in an age when the horse was a means of travel.

Mooball: Possibly meaning lake, swamp or lagoon.

Murwillumbah: A much disputed name generally taken to mean the place of many possums. Aboriginal in derivation.

Nardi (Mount): Named after a councillor of Terania shire.

Nightcap Range: Commonly called the Nightcaps the name is believed to be a corruption of the term night camp.

Nimbin: Aboriginal for wise man.

Numinbah: Aboriginal for holding tight.

O'Reillys: The mountain resort operated by the O'Reilly family on the edge of the Lamington National Park. The official name is Green Mountains.

Oxley River: The middle arm of the Tweed River named after the explorer John Oxley.

Pinnacle (The): A descriptive name, sometimes called the Tweed Pinnacle to distinguish it from other similar features such as Lofts Pinnacle a few kilometres directly west.

Point Lookout: A descriptive name.

Pumpenbil: Aboriginal said to refer to a tree.

Rawson Island: Named for a governor of NSW.

Rous River: The north arm of the Tweed River named after the explorer Henry Rous.

Stotts Island: Named after an early settler and former convict James Stott.

Tarrawyra (Mount): Possible Aboriginal derivation from the words for either running water or loose stones.

Terania (Creek): From the Aboriginal for frog.

Throakban (Mount): From the Aboriginal for echo.

Tomewin: A curious name probably derived from the name of local haulier Tom Windley. (Tom-e-Win or Tommy Win?)

Tooloona (Mount): Aboriginal for frilled lizard.

Tumbulgum: Aboriginal for the small-leafed fig. Commonly believed to mean meeting of the waters.

Tuntable: Derived from the word turn table.

Tyalgum: Believed to be Aboriginal for tall timbers.

Uki: Aboriginal for a small water plant with edible roots.

Wagawn: One of surveyor Roberts' names from the Aboriginal for crow.

Wannungra (Mount): Meaning unknown probably Aboriginal in derivation.

Warning (Mount): Named by Captain Cook on 15 May 1770 after an escape from dangerous shoals off the coast.

Whian Whian: Aboriginal for a tree with large roots that can furnish a little shelter (possibly an old blackbutt).

Wiangarie: Aboriginal for camping place.

Wollumbin: The Aboriginal name for Mt Warning said to mean high mountain or cloud maker.

Woodenbong: Aboriginal for a lagoon.

Worendo (Mount): Aboriginal for fast flowing.

Wupan (Mount): Aboriginal for smart or clever.

(Readers will note that the Aboriginal names are not accurate descriptions of places. This may result from misunderstandings by the white interpreters or from the Aboriginal association of features with mythological events or beings)

APPENDIX 2
PLANT—SCIENTIFIC CLASSIFICATION

Common Name	Family	Genus	Species
Antarctic beech	Fagaceae	*Nothofagus*	*moorei*
Bangalow palm	Palmae	*Archontophoenix*	*cunninghamiana*
beech orchid	Orchidaceae	*Dendrobium*	*falcorostrum*
bird's-nest fern	Aspleniaceae	*Asplenium*	*australasicium*
black apple	Sapotaceae	*Planchonella*	*australis*
blady grass	Poaceae	*Imperata*	*cylindrica*
bloodwood (pink)	Myrtaceae	*Eucalyptus*	*intermedia*
blue fig (quandong)	Elaeocarpaceae	*Elaeocarpus*	*grandis*
brush box	Myrtaceae	*Tristania*	*conferta*
callicoma	Cunoniaceae	*Callicoma*	*serratifolia*
coachwood	Cunoniaceae	*Ceropetalum*	*apetalum*
crab apple	Cunoniaceae	*Schizomeria*	*ovata*
crofton weed	Compositae	*Eupatorium*	*adenophorum*
cunjevoi	Araceae	*Alocasia*	*macrorrhizos*
elk horn fern	Polypodiaceae	*Platycerium*	*bifurcatum*
flame tree	Sterculiaceae	*Brachychiton*	*acerifolium*
flooded gum	Myrtaceae	*Eucalyptus*	*grandis*
forest oak	Casuarinaceae	*Casuarina*	*torulosa*
giant stinging tree	Urticaceae	*Dendrocnide*	*excelsa*
giant water gum	Myrtaceae	*Syzygium*	*francisii*
giant water vine	Vitidaceae	*Cissus* sp.	
grasstree	Xanthorrhoeaceae	*Xanthorrhoea* sp.	
grey gum	Myrtaceae	*Eucalyptus*	*punctata*
grey ironbark	Myrtaceae	Eucalyptus	siderophloia
hoop pine	Araucariaceae	*Araucaria*	*cunninghamii*
kangaroo grass	Poaceae	*Themeda*	*australis*
lantana	Verbenaceae	*Lantana*	*camara*
lawyer cane (vine)	Palmae	*Calamus*	*muelleri*
lemon-scented tea-tree	Myrtaceae	*Leptospermum*	*petersonii*

Common Name	Family	Genus	Species
lilly pilly	Myrtaceae	*Acmena*	*smithii*
macadamia nut	Proteaceae	*Macadamia*	*tetraphylla*
midginbil	Palmae	*Linospadix*	*monostachyus*
Moreton bay fig	Moraceae	*Ficus*	*macrophylla*
native tamarind	Sapindaceae	*Diploglottis*	*australis*
New England blackbutt	Myrtaceae	*Eucalyptus*	*andrewsii*
northern gymea lily	Agavaceae	*Doryanthes*	*palmeri*
python tree	Myrtaceae	*Austromyrtus*	*bidwillii*
red cedar	Meliaceae	*Toona*	*australis*
rock orchid	Orchidaceae	*Liparis*	*reflexa*
rose marara	Cunoniaceae	*Pseudoweinmannia*	*lachnocarpa*
rosewood	Meliaceae	*Dysoxylum*	*fraseranum*
stag horn fern	Polpodiaceae	*Platycerium*	*grande*
strangler fig	Moraceae	*Ficus*	*watkinsiana*
Sydney blue gum	Myrtaceae	*Eucalyptus*	*saligna*
tallow wood	Myrtaceae	*Eucalyptus*	*microcorys*
tree fern (prickley)	Cyatheaceae	*Cyathea*	*leichardtiana*
turpentine	Myrtaceae	*Syncarpia*	*glomulifera*
white booyong	Sterculiaceae	*Heritiera*	*trifoliolata*
white mahogany	Myrtaceae	*Eucalyptus*	*acmenioides*
wild ginger	Zingiberaceae	*Alpinea*	*caerulea*
yellow tea-tree	Myrtaceae	*Leptospermum*	*flavescens*

APPENDIX 3
FAUNA—SCIENTIFIC CLASSIFICATION

Common name	Scientific name

BIRDS

Albert lyrebird	*Menura alberti*
brown pigeon	*Macropygia amboinensis*
brush turkey (scrub turkey)	*Alectura lathami*
butcher bird	*Cracticus nigrogularis*
catbird	*Ailuroedus crassirostris*
crimson rosella	*Platycercus elegans*
emerald dove	*Chalcophaps indica*
top knot pigeon	*Lopholaimus antarcticus*
red-crowned pigeon (rose crowned fruit dove)	*Ptilinopus regina*
regent bowerbird	*Sericulus chrysocephalus*
rufous scrub-bird	*Atrichornis rufescens*
satin bowerbird	*Ptilonorhynchus violaceus*
wompoo pigeon (magnificent fruit dove)	*Ptilinopus magnificus*
whipbird (eastern)	*Psophodes olivaceus*

BUTTERFLIES

big greasy	*Cressida cressida cressida*
capaneus	*Papilio fuscus capaneus*
four-bar swordtail	*Protographium leosthenes*
pale green triangle	*Graphium eurypylus*
regent skipper	*Euschemon rafflesia*
Richmond River birdwing	*Ornithoptera richmondia*

Common name	Scientific name

MAMMALS

MONOTREMES
echidna	*Tachyglossus aculeatus*

MARSUPIALS

bandicoot (long-nosed)	*Perameles nasuta*
dusky marsupial mouse	*Antechinus swainsonii*
gliders—greater	*Petauroides volans*
—squirrel	*Petaurus norfolcensis*
—sugar	*Petaurus breviceps*
koala	*Phascolarctos cinereus*
pademelon (red-necked)	*Thylogale thetis*
possum—brushtail	*Trichosurus vulpecula*
—mountain	*Trichosurus caninus*
—ringtail	*Pseudocheirus perigrinus*
Tiger-quoll	*Dasyurus maculatus*
wallabies—red-necked	*Macropus rufogriseus*
—whiptail	*Macropus parryi*
—parma	*Macropus parma*

PLACENTALS

flying fox (black)	*Pteropus alecto*
dingo	*Canis familiaris dingo*

REPTILES

black snake (red-bellied)	*Pseudechis porphyriacus*
carpet snake	*Morelai spilota*
goanna(lace monitor)	*Varanus varius*
land mullet	*Egernia major*
rough scale (tiger snake)	*Notechis scutatus*
rough scale snake	*Notechis scutatus*

Common name	Scientific name

FROGS

Loveridge's frog	*Philoria loveridgei*
pouched frog	*Assa darlingtoni*
giant barred frog	*Mixophyes iteratus*

OTHERS

eel (long-finned)	*Anguilla reinhardtii*
leech	*Haemadipsoidae* spp.
crayfish (Lamington blue)	*Euastacus* sp.

APPENDIX 4
GLOSSARY OF TERMS

agglomerate: A type of acid volcanic rock composed of varied particle sizes. Usually associated with explosive volcanic activity.

aplite dyke: An acid volcanic intrusion of light-coloured igneous rock similar in composition to rhyolite.

basalt: Basic volcanic lava which flows readily creating shield-type formations. Basalt produces fertile soils.

big scrub: The local name for an area of lowland subtropical rainforest formerly located on the basalt hills between Bangalow and Lismore.

blaze: A trail marker. In the past blazes were cut in the bark of trees, nowadays it is more usual to use removable plastic tape.

buttress: Tree roots up to 3 metres above the ground, standing out from the trunk of the tree yet connected to the trunk. Function unknown.

caldera: A large circular depression at the centre of a volcano. The normal caldera is produced by the collapse of the centre of the volcano after the lava flow stops and no longer provides support.

canopy: The relatively continuous cover created by the interlocking crowns of rainforest trees.

central vent: The pipe through which a central volcano extrudes its lava.

claystones: Sedimentary rocks created by the solidification of deposits of clay under pressure over a considerable period of time.

community: A group of plants which not only share a particular environment but are in other ways dependent upon each other.

coppicing: A method of reproduction whereby a tree sends up new shoots from the old rootstock.

depauperate: Impoverished or reduced in value. With respect to plant communities usually means reduced in species numbers or vigour. Results from disturbance by natural causes (fires, wind etc.) or human activity.

diorite: A coarse-grained intermediate volcanic rock somewhat similar to granite, diorite is formed when lava cools beneath the surface.

dry sclerophyll: Sclerophyll forests are composed in the main of eucalypts and acacias, the dry sclerophyll forests are recognisable for their less dense canopy and the resultant relatively dense ground cover of grasses and shrubs.

dyke: A vertical intrusion of molten lava into an existing rock layer.

ecogeologic unit: A term used by the authors to describe the close relationship between geology, flora and the associated fauna in the Tweed volcano remnants.

ecology: The study of the relationship between various sections of the natural environment.

elkhorn: An epiphyte, actually a fern, with thin ribbon-like leaves protruding from the base somewhat reminiscent of antlers.

epiphytes: 'Air plants', plants which exist without contact with soil. These 'perch' on rocks or trees and have special adaptations which allow them to collect and process leaf litter into food. Some typical examples are the crows nest fern, the staghorn, and the elkhorn.

erosion caldera: A circular hollow created as erosion exploits the weakness of the junction between the hard rock of a volcanic plug and the softer extruded lavas and ashes. Similar in shape to a normal caldera but different in its genesis.

extrusive: Volcanic rocks which reach the surface and cool above ground.

fire refuge: An area protected from fire. Plants susceptible to fire may persist in such areas long after fire has eliminated them from surrounding fire-prone areas.

gabbro: A coarse-grained volcanic rock similar to basalt but formed below the surface where the process of cooling takes longer and the rock crystals have more time to develop.

gorge: A deeply incised valley with sheer or very steeply sloping sides.

greywacke: A type of grey metamorphosed sandstone.

heath: A vegetation type which features smaller trees and shrubs mixed with coarse grasses. Usually found on poor soils or environments in some way deficient.

interfluve: The area of higher ground separating two streams. Often called a divide or drainage divide.

intrusive: Volcanic rocks which solidify beneath the ground in magma chambers, vents or cracks in the Earth's surface.

krasnozem: A rich red loam soil associated with basalt parent material.

lava: The material extruded from the vent in a volcano. Lava may be of the fluid basic variety (basalt) or the thick 'gluggy' acid variety (rhyolite).

mangroves: Salt-water tolerant trees which grow on the margins of coastal swamps and river banks.

metamorphic: Rocks which are radically altered by heat and pressure.

palm glade: An area in the rainforest dominated by palm trees. In the Tweed they are usually bangalow palms.

phyllites: A type of metamorphic rock often quarried for road base in the Tweed area.

pillow lava: A 'lumpy' lava flow caused by the cooling of the lava in water. The lumps are in the general shape of a pillow.

plateau: An area of relatively level but elevated land at least one edge of which is steeply sloping.

plug: The lava which solidifies in the vent of a volcano on its extinction. This material is usually more resistant to erosion than the surrounding extruded material. It is sometimes called a plug or core.

podzolic: A poor type of soil which has had the soluble plant foods and smaller particles washed deep below the surface. In areas which have coarse-grained parent material they often have a sandy ash grey upper horizon. On the sedimentary rocks of the Tweed which have little sandy material they do not exhibit this feature.

radial drainage: Where the streams draining an area radiate out from the centre like the spokes in a wheel.

rhyolite: An acid lava which forms the cliff lines around the Tweed Valley. Rhyolite is usually associated with violent volcanic activity.

ria: A deep coastal inlet created when a rise in sea level floods the lower parts of a river valley, for example Sydney harbour.

ring dyke: A dyke is a layer of volcanic material which is forced vertically into cracks in the overlying rocks. Mt Warning has a series of dykes which form a ring around its lower slopes.

sandstones: Rocks composed of sand particles of sedimentary origin. These rocks are very porous and readily allow water to penetrate and pass through them.

sedimentary: Rocks which are transported to an area by wind or water as separate grains and are later cemented together.

staghorns: An epiphyte, actually a fern, with an outer leaf which almost covers the whole plant in a manner somewhat similar to a lettuce. Similar to and often confused with elkhorns.

subtropical rainforest: Forest having similar structure to the tropical rainforest but being located in cooler areas and having different species.

temperate rainforest: Forest having a rainforest structure but being located in cooler areas. Its species are different to those of the subtropical rainforests and are closely related to southern floras. Temperate rainforests are found on the cooler mountain tops in the Tweed district.

terraces: Raised areas of former flood plain located on the margins of present flood plains. Where they result from different rock types they are called structural terraces.

tor: A large rounded boulder left behind when deep weathering and erosion remove the surrounding material. Common in granite landscapes.

trachyte: A dense erosion-resistant rock formed as lava solidifies within the vent of a volcano producing acid lavas.

tuff: A rock type composed of solidified ash from an explosive phase of a volcanic vent producing acid lava.

understorey: The layer of plants on the floor of a forest, below the canopy.

vents: Holes from which lava is extruded from a volcano during eruptions.

viny scrub: A form of depauperate rainforest resulting from past destruction of natural rainforest.

volcanic shield: A large relatively flat landscape formed by successive flows of fast-flowing basic (basaltic) lavas.

volcano: The landform created by lava as it wells up from inside the Earth's crust. Not all volcanoes are of the picture postcard variety which are created by acid lavas. Many are far less spectacular, Mt Warning, for example would have been much larger but far less impressive than it is today at the peak of its development.

water table: The upper surface of the saturated lower sections of the soil.

wet sclerophyll: A type of forest dominated by eucalypts but having a dense canopy and much less ground cover than its drier relative.

yellow earths: Podzolic soils in the Tweed area created by the washing of plant foods and fine material out of the upper layers of the soil but not having the sandy layer normally associated with podzolic soils.

APPENDIX 5
SELECT BIBLIOGRAPHY

Brouwer, Steven (ed.) *Message of Terania*. Terania Media. 1980.

Davies, Wally. *Richmond Tweed Wildlife Survey—— Guidebook for Observers*. Big Scrub Environmental Centre. 1986.

Graham, B.W. 'Landform Development of the Tweed Area'. Unpublished notes from adult education lectures. Undated.

Forestry Commission (NSW). *Environmental Impact Statement for Border Ranges*. NSW Forestry Commission.

Forestry Commission (NSW). *Environmental Impact Statement Terania Creek Basin*. NSW Forestry Commission.

Groom, Arthur. *One Mountain After Another*. Angus & Robertson. 1967.

Groom, Tony & Gynther, Trevor. *One Hundred Walks in South Queensland*. Hill of Content. Melbourne. 1980.

National Parks. *Mt Warning National Park—Draft Plan of Management*. National Parks & Wildlife Service NSW. May 1985.

Nicholson, Nan & Hugh. *Australian Rainforest Plants*. Terania Rainforest Nursery. 1985.

Nicholson, Nan & Hugh. *Australian Rainforest Plants Vol. 2*. Terania Rainforest Nursery. 1985.

O'Reilly, Bernard. *Green Mountains and Cullenbenbong*. Smith & Paterson Pty Ltd. 1949.

O'Reilly, Bernard. *Over the Hills*. Smith & Paterson Pty Ltd. 1963.

Richmond Valley Naturalists Club & Lismore Gem & Mineral Society. *Geological Feature of the Richmond Valley*. 1975.

Richmond–Tweed Regional Library. *Place Names of the Tweed, Brunswick and Upper Richmond Regions*. Richmond–Tweed Regional Library. 1984.

Yuile, Mark. 'The Search for the Stinson'. Australian Wilderness Magazine *Wild*. vol.7, no.3, 1987.

INDEX

(Excluding appendices)